SHUT UP!

Stop Talking and Start Making Money

I hope you enjoy the book, Gary!

Dave

Dave Warawa - PROSALESGUY

www.prosalesguy.ca

Library and Archives Canada Cataloguing in Publication

Warawa, David, 1962-, author
    Shut up! Stop talking and start making money / David Warawa.

ISBN 978-1-5003-2137-6 (pbk.)

    1. Selling. 2. Selling--Handbooks, manuals, etc.
I. Title.

HF5438.25.W355 2014   658.85   C2014-905431-9

Editing: Ryan Parton Writing Solutions
Cover Photos: Seadance Photography
Cover Design and Layout: The Writer Connection

This book is dedicated to everyone that I've had the privilege of working with over 30 years – co-workers, Professional Salespeople, sales managers, general managers, business owners and decision-makers.

Without you, this book would not be possible.

Many thanks to my wonderful wife Tammy, who tolerated me throughout the writing of this book. She eagerly volunteered to zip my mouth shut for the front cover.

Stop! Is this book for you?

Before you seriously consider buying this book, please read this to ensure you're making the right purchase.

Who is this book designed for?

I've written this book for Professional Salespeople, sales managers, business owners and anyone interested in making more sales – either for themselves or for their organization. It will also be extremely valuable to anyone wishing to become skilled in the art of persuading, motivating and leading people.

 In my experience, the most powerful and rewarding success skill is *the ability to relate to people.* Follow the advice in this book, become a master of this one key skill and you're virtually guaranteed to achieve success – both in business and in your personal life.

Why would you buy it?

This book is the culmination of more than 30 years of business experience as a Professional Salesperson, sales manager, trainer and consultant. Over my career, I've been fortunate to have sold real estate, life insurance door-to-door and media advertising, and I've been a radio and television broadcaster.

I'm a career salesperson. I'm proud of my profession. I love helping other motivated salespeople become Sales Superstars.

My Dream

After years working for many great companies, I finally decided to pursue two life-long ambitions:

 ✓ Become self-employed as an independent sales trainer and business consultant.

✓ Capture a career worth of sales experiences in a book to help other salespeople improve.

Those ambitions, both of which I've now fulfilled, represent two of the toughest experiences of my entire career. They've also been two of the most rewarding. There's nothing quite like experiencing your dreams.

What's *your* calling?

Mark Twain once wrote "the two most important days in your life are the day you are born and the day you find out why."

I'm very fortunate to have found my calling. We all deserve the chance to be great at what we do, and I wrote this book to give you the opportunity to stand on the shoulders of my sales experience. If you're a Professional Salesperson, or want the skill set of one, then this book is for you.

INTRODUCTION
Will you read this book?

The mere fact that you're reading this suggests that you've determined this book is worth your time and money. Thanks for your faith in me. Now let's get right to your first lesson:

There's a difference between salespeople and Professional Salespeople. It rests with one word:

Professional

What do we expect professionals to do? What do we expect from doctors, lawyers, accountants, airline pilots and anyone else we hold in high regard?

 We expect professionals to make a commitment toward a high standard of quality in education, expertise, ability and *continual improvement*.

We've all heard of the 80/20 rule. In sales, it's more like 90/10. *90% of sales commissions are made by the top 10% of Professional Salespeople.* That leaves only 10% of the income left for 90% of salespeople to battle over. Here's why it happens:

The "accidental" salesperson

Many people have had bad experiences with salespeople and believe the profession has little credibility. They think sales is what you do if you don't have a college education or university degree.

Too many salespeople stumbled into the profession because a colleague, friend or family member told them at some point that they have the "right personality" for the job. Their only real "training" has been personal experience. *What if that experience has been bad?*

Sink-or-swim is for waterlogged kittens, not salespeople

For most salespeople who *have* completed some sort of sales training, it's been a one-day seminar with no field application. Sales managers often think sink-or-swim is the best way to determine good salespeople – after all, it's what they were told when they started in the business.

The rhetorical question I hear most often from sales managers in defense of their unwillingness to train their sales teams goes something like this: *"What happens if I train my salespeople and they leave for the competition?"*

 My reply is this:

"What happens if you don't and they stay?"

Are YOU a Professional?

Professional salespeople don't merely "end up" in sales. They choose their career and make a conscious decision to continually improve.

Unfortunately, after working in the sales industry for more than 30 years, I've realized that only a small minority of salespeople will read a book that would allow them to better their skill set, improve their incomes and feel better about their profession. That's an incredibly unfortunate, sad statement to make.

The problem certainly isn't due to a lack of resources. There are hundreds of great books from qualified authors that are easily accessible through technology, your local bookshop and even second-hand stores. I've seen some of the best books in the industry, written by Professional Salespeople like Tom Hopkins, Brian Tracy, Jeffrey Gitomer and the late Zig Ziglar, at second-hand bookstores for as little as a dollar.

So why don't salespeople read more?

We live in a fast-paced society with too much to do and too little time to do it. Like most modern-day professionals, salespeople are busy multi-tasking between work and family commitments. That leaves far too many of us feeling as if we don't have the time to learn better techniques to improve our skill set. What precious time we have, we reason, should be dedicated to chasing commissions, not reading books.

Is it a lack of time or lack of priority?

Let's be honest and direct. *We can all make personal improvement a priority*. It's as simple as *creating* the time for it. Think of the time you spend flipping through television channels complaining that there's nothing decent to watch. How about the hours devoted to Facebook or silly videos on YouTube? Though staying connected with friends and being entertained is great, could you not sacrifice a few minutes each week to better yourself?

Here's your challenge: **devote 15 minutes of every day to reading**. Before long, as you begin to realize the tangible effects that continual improvement has on your career and on your life, I guarantee it will grow to 30.

Read one great book every three months and you'll gain the knowledge of four books each year. Your sales are guaranteed to improve! Your confidence will increase, your skill set will improve and you'll be open to new, creative ideas. Best of all, you'll feel pride in being among the top 10% of Professional Salespeople.

Oh, and here are two more things you can expect as a Professional Salesperson:

1. **Your monthly paycheques will increase.**

2. **You'll experience a better standard for living for you and your family.**

 And all it takes is a simple commitment to read for 15 minutes each day.

So here's my question:

Will you read this book?

If so, I have another task for you. As you read this book, highlight the sections that you really like. Every three months, go back and reread your highlighted sections, which will reinforce the areas that made the most impact on you. It's like power-reading the entire book in 15 minutes and will drive home the most important lessons.

I'll see you at the top!

CHAPTER 1
The Stigma of Sales

Tell people at a dinner party that you're a salesperson and one of two things happens. They either say *"Oh yeah?"* and start looking for a way to get away from you or they ask the famous question, *"So, how would you sell ice to an Eskimo?"*

Really? Is that what society thinks of our profession? Unfortunately, yes.

I once asked the following question on my weekly **PROSALESGUY BLOG** (www.prosalesguy.ca/blog):

What is the first word that comes to mind when you hear the word "salesperson"?

The top three words that came back were:

1. *Pushy*

2. *Persistent*

3. *Peddler*

These were followed by *Slick, Aggressive, Annoying, Arrogant, Avoided, Caution, Cheesy, Closer, Cost, Crafty, Dishonest, Evil, Greedy, Intrusive, Lying, Mover, No, Relentless, Scumbag, Shady, Snake-oil, Suspicious, Talker, Tricky and Unprepared.*

Suddenly there's little mystery why so many people avoid careers in sales. The entire profession carries a horrible stigma.

When I later sent the same request to select colleagues and associates within the sales industry, I received an entirely different set of words:

Advisor, Achiever, Awesome, Believer, Brilliant, Communicator, Confident, Consistent, Detailed, Diligent, Ethical, Facilitator, Firefighter, Flexible, Focused, Great, Hardworking, Helpful, Honest, Inquisitive, Listener, Passionate, Persevering, Personable, Resourceful, Service, Solvers, Trustworthy, Vibrant, Work Hard

Now, *that's* more like it!

There is an elite group of Professional Salespeople within our industry who are proud of what they do and to whom the idea of selling ice to an Eskimo is a ridiculous test of sales ability. By working hard to offer their customers the very best in service and resourcefulness they've earned those capital letters in their title of "Professional Salesperson."

So where's the disconnect?

 Salespeople spend far too much time trying to sell products and services to people who don't want to buy them. Instead of chasing after people, Professional Salespeople invest their time *sourcing out* those future customers who are actively looking for their product or service. Then, rather than delivering a longwinded sales pitch, they provide *education* so that the prospect can make a genuinely beneficial decision. *That's* how you get repeat business and *that's* how you earn referrals.

Closing techniques are seldom required when you're speaking with qualified prospects with a genuine interest in what you have to offer. Such prospects will exhibit the buying signs that make their intentions clear. "When can I start?" "How quick is delivery?" "What form of down payment is required?" "What payment methods do you offer?" These all indicate a high interest in making a purchase.

The ABCs of sales is NOT Always Be Closing!

 In the movie Glengarry Glen Ross, Alec Baldwin plays an overbearing sales manager who is so obnoxious and vile that he doesn't even have a name. The Salespeople at his real estate company are browbeaten and abused in the hope that such humiliation will sufficiently motivate them to sell people regardless of their needs or desires.

Baldwin's character subscribes to the sales mantra of "Always Be Closing." "Get them to sign on the line that is dotted" is just one of the often-quoted lines from the film. While the movie fell shy of expectations with the general public, it's a cult classic within the sales industry and is a shining example of what not to do and how not to act.

The real ABCs of sales

The true ABCs of sales is Always Be Connecting. Smart salespeople are always connecting with their current customers and reaching out to establish new relationships. They don't take their clients' business for granted and they're always looking for new opportunities.

How to treat new customers

Professional Salespeople are always looking to establish new revenue streams. Cancellations, attrition and buyer's remorse are realities of the sales profession. As a wise mentor once told me, "the sale is not made until the cheque clears the bank." Every Sales Superstar with whom I've had the pleasure of working has experienced at least one decimating sales slump during which they questioned their future in sales.

Too many salespeople become proactive only when faced with *dire necessity*. Instead, be proactive consistently – *especially* when you don't need to be. That's how you grow your business, your confidence, your experience and your paycheque. It sure beats going into a panicked "new business acquisition" mode every time you notice a dip in your commissions.

How to treat existing customers

Professional Salespeople service and maintain their loyal customers to the same degree they did before they started buying. How does it make you feel when a salesperson courts you, closes the deal and then moves on to the next prospect? Probably like the girl who was asked for a date on Thursday night and not called again after the weekend. If you can keep the vast majority of your current customers happy, and continually buying, then there's less pressure on you to develop new customers.

The impressions salespeople can give their customers

We've already seen what the general public thinks about salespeople. Here's a few commonly shared beliefs:

Salespeople are friendly and caring only because of their personal agenda to make a sale.
Salespeople care more about their pocketbook than my best interest.
You can get rid of a salesperson by showing little desire to buy or ability to pay.

Salespeople fuss all over you to make a sale and then disappear after the purchase.
After the sale is made, the relationship with the salesperson ends until I show interest to buy again.
Watch out for great salespeople; they'll take your last dollar.

Wow, little wonder our industry has an imaging problem.

What customers *really* want

Just treat me with respect and you'll get it back.
Look out for my best interest and your chances of getting a repeat sale greatly increase.
If I buy based on liking you and your product, I'll send my friends over to ask for you personally.
Really impress me and I'll share my experience on social media.
Really annoy me and I'll do the same.
Please understand that I will have to buy this product again in the future.
I want to buy repeatedly from the same salesperson and company because I hate looking for new ones.

That sounds much better, doesn't it?

Professional Salespeople increase their odds of an upsell or repeat purchase when they invest in maintaining an authentic, sincere relationship with their buyers. Just play nice and you will see the return.

Why does the stigma of sales exist?

I'm convinced that this lies at the core of the problem. The stigma of 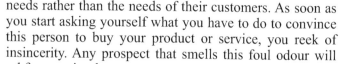 sales will survive as long as salespeople focus on their own needs rather than the needs of their customers. As soon as you start asking yourself what you have to do to convince this person to buy your product or service, you reek of insincerity. Any prospect that smells this foul odour will walk away, and for one simple reason:

Lack of Trust

If I don't trust you, I won't buy from you. Even if you have the best product, service or offer, I will not do business with you because I don't like you. I will travel across town and even resort to buying a less appealing product from a Professional Salesperson who doesn't have his or her hand in my pocket. If I feel that your needs as a salesperson, or the needs of your company, come before mine, then I'm going to say goodbye. I'm not interested.

What's your agenda?

The most effective agenda you can have as a Professional Salesperson is unbelievably simple. *Help your customers.* Don't focus on making a sale. Concentrate on educating people to allow them to make decisions that will benefit *them.* In every industry in which I've worked, the market leader in educating their customers has also been the market leader in sales. They achieve sales growth through credibility.

My personal sales philosophy

If someone had told me at the start of my career that I was going to be a Professional Salesperson, sales manager and eventually a sales trainer, I would have laughed until I cried. *I had no respect for salespeople.* Like most people, I thought they were the type of people that would sell their own mother for the right commission.

When I realized that being successful in sales was about *helping* people rather than *selling* them, a light came on for me, and I was able to formulate my personal sales philosophy:

My job is to give people the information they need to make good decisions. The more information they have, the better the decisions they'll make.

This philosophy became my mandate and my agenda. Once my customers understood this, they liked me. They trusted me. They bought from me. Then they bought from me again. Then they sent their friends to me.

The sales profession doesn't need to have a stigma. It can be a great, respected career choice for many young professionals who are up for a challenge and are motivated by the satisfaction of helping others.

I'm proud to be a Professional Salesperson, sales manager and sales trainer because I bring class to the industry. *What do you bring?*

CHAPTER 2
The Most Common Mistakes Salespeople Make

Success comes from a combination of avoiding what you know doesn't work, repeating what you know does work and dedicating the time to learn the difference. Mistakes are inevitable. Learning from those mistakes is a key quality of Professional Salespeople.

Here are the most common mistakes we've all made as salespeople:

Talk too much

 You've probably already guessed from the title of this book that I'm not a fan of salespeople who don't know when to shut up. It's a cliché that salespeople need to have the gift of gab. We already know what society thinks of salespeople, so avoiding this pitfall is a smart move. Talking too much, in fact, is probably THE biggest mistake salespeople make.

We've all encountered a salesperson who just won't stop yapping, and we all hate it. Correct me if I'm wrong! Rather than listening to what he or she is saying, we're left dumbstruck, wondering how they manage to breathe considering that their lips never stop moving.

An over-talkative salesperson is typically the sign of either someone who has just started in the industry or a salesperson who has never had any training. Trying to get your prospect to the point of "I'll buy if you just stop talking" is not a smart technique.

Please just shut up already! If you think that's rude, understand that it's exactly what customers are thinking about you.

Don't follow-up

 This is another huge problem with salespeople. We all want to make a sale and we live for the moment when a prospect becomes a customer. It's the ultimate vote of approval. It means you did a great job, and that your client likes you and trusts you. Your sales manager will be happy with your performance and the general manager might even acknowledge you with a smile in the hallway. That's not even considering the fact that you work in an industry where your work ethic and performance directly translates into higher pay.

We often place so much importance on making a sale, though, that we tend to move on quickly when we don't get one immediately. We scurry off to the next possible customer knowing that the more people we talk to, the better the chance of making a sale. It's a numbers game, right? Wrong.

Salespeople are quick to forget that timing is everything when it comes to making a purchase. A shopper is someone who is considering a purchase and needs more time and information to make a final decision. A buyer is someone who has already made that decision.

A prospect not ready to buy today is a customer who may still want to buy at some point in the future. Salespeople feel the two are the same. Professional Salespeople understand the difference. Follow up with prospects and ask them two important questions:

1. *Is there any more information I could provide you?*

2. *When might I be able to give you a friendly call to follow-up with you? What time of day is best to reach you, and at what number?*

OK, so technically that was four questions. When you get your prospect's answer, write it in your planner or enter it on your Smartphone and call them *on the exact day and at the exact time agreed to.* When you do, remind them that you're calling because *they* said it was a good time to call. No need to sweat over fabricating a thinly veiled "reason" for the call – you already have the best one!

It's shocking to think how many sales are lost because salespeople give prospects the impression that they're all about the quick sale. Professional Salespeople develop a relationship before the sale is made. That attracts people to you and makes them want to commit.

Take rejection personally

As a salesperson, rejection is inevitable. Taking it personally is another sure sign of a rookie salesperson. Sales is for the tough-minded and thick-skinned. If you don't find a way to deal with rejection, *you will not last long in this industry.* Here's a little secret: When a prospect says "No," what they're really saying is:

"I'm not interested in what you have to offer at this given point in time."

That's a lot of words, which is why simply saying "No" is a lot easier. Timing is crucial in the sales process. Someone who says "No" today could be saying "Yes" next week when something in their world changes. This is why following up and establishing a relationship before the purchase is key to making future sales.

When I sold life insurance door-to-door, my goal was to simply get an appointment. Out of 10 people I talked to, seven would say "No thank you," one would say "No" and close the door in my face and one would say "No" in a much less polite fashion. One, however, might be willing to book an appointment. Here was my character-building philosophy: The more I heard "No," the closer I was getting to "Yes." I learned a lot from that Professional Sales opportunity.

Look for shortcuts

There are no shortcuts.

There is no way to beat the system of being successful in sales. It takes hard work sustained over a long period of time.

I remember one year that one of my media Sales Superstars – let's call him James – achieved record sales. Even though I knew the answer anyway, I asked him what led to his incredible year. Here's what he said:

"I don't know Dave. I came to work every day, got on the phone to make appointments, did a complete needs analysis, put together a strategy based on their needs and objectives and confirmed the business. I worked hard with my clients throughout the year to make sure I never took them for granted and I always brought forward new ideas. I didn't do anything other than what you trained me to do."

Get the picture? James did. There are no shortcuts.

Focus on price

Our clients and prospects tell us that price is everything. They want the best quality product for the lowest possible price, and they expect you to provide incredible service to boot. That's a formula for bankruptcy. Every company needs to make a healthy profit in order to stay in business and provide employment.

Ask yourself this question:

If buyers are only interested in price, why don't you hear them bragging about the great deal they got on a piece of junk?

Price is what you pay; value is what you get. We'll dive into that later in the book. For now, just know that discounts and price reductions are a slippery slope that someone else is always prepared to beat you on.

Deal with the wrong people

 As salespeople, we've all spent way too much time with the wrong people. Sometimes it's unavoidable. Screeners and administrative assistants have the task of compiling information and reporting to a buyer or senior purchasing agent. The key is finding out who the real decision maker(s) is after the first appointment. How do you do that? With this one carefully worded question:

"Who, besides yourself, is involved in or responsible for making the final decision?"

I would be careful to ask that at the *end* of the first meeting. If asked at the start, here's what your prospect will hear:

"Who do I have to talk to to get a decision made, since it's obviously not you?"

Make that mistake and you will not get a second chance.

Panic prospecting

 This is what salespeople do when experiencing customer attrition or when expected sales fall through. They realize they're in big trouble and go into panic prospecting mode immediately for several hours each day. They attempt to speed up the sales process and try to pick the low-lying fruit that isn't even ripe. This gives your prospects and clients the impression that you're desperate for sales and are not keeping their best interests at heart.

Professional Salespeople prospect for new lines of business *all the time*.

This results in record years and makes attrition a virtual non-factor. It also lessens the impact of tough years, as the bite of lost business is not as deep.

Making assumptions

"This client won't be interested in this product line." "This prospect is not suited to my offer." "I know what my clients need." "She will never pay that much."

How many of these kinds of assumptions have you been guilty of making? Though you may know your client well, always do a check-up to make sure nothing has changed since you last talked. Don't EVER assume that the needs of one client are the wants of many. Ask. Check. Stay open-minded.

Lying by omission

The late Zig Ziglar was a master of this topic. He felt that if your job as a Professional Salesperson is to educate your potential buyer, then you can't leave out specific details. Lack of disclosure is the cousin of lying. Give your prospect all the information that is necessary to make an educated choice.

Omitting a pertinent detail is usually a symptom of an agenda that's not in the prospect's best interest. If you're asked, *"Why didn't you tell me that before?"* answering with, *"You didn't ask"* will almost certainly lose the sale.

Not having a system

Professional Salespeople strategize. They observe those who have had success. They ask for opinions and guidance. They put together a sales system that serves as a business plan for their activities. They fully commit to their system, ask their sales managers for help when needed and follow their plan with discipline and persistence.

Professional Salespeople are masters of the art of delayed gratification. Too many salespeople "wing it," trying different things each week as if searching for the Holy Grail that will make them a Sales Superstar overnight. If that sounds like you, it's time to end your quest for the Holy Grail. Like King Arthur, you're not going to find it.

CHAPTER 3
The Four C's of Learning New Sales Techniques

Throughout this book, you'll be presented with many new sales techniques that have been proven to work. It's up to you to learn them, practise them and internalize them. If you do, you'll be well on your way to becoming a Sales Superstar.

Learning new sales techniques is something Professional Salespeople strive to do continually. Whether you've just started in the industry or have many years of experience, being open-minded and willing to try new self-improvement methods is part of your career journey.

My observations

I've seen many salespeople quickly abandon a new technique because it doesn't work for them. Yet there are also many examples of the exact opposite, where the new method works successfully and quickly becomes part of a regular routine. Why does this occur with such wildly different results?

After learning from hundreds of salespeople over 30 years, I've observed that there are four C's of learning a new sales technique.

The first C: Comfort

This tends to be the primary reason why a new procedure doesn't work. Allow me to give you an example:

When I started in my sales career many years ago, I read of a new technique in prospecting by phone. Typically, you often hear this objection when you call a new potential prospect to try to book an appointment:

"I'm not interested in what you have to offer."

'Here's the suggested response that I'd read about:

"I realize that. If you were, you would've called me. I'm simply calling you to see if we can get together for 30 minutes. I'm not even sure if my product is suited to your business. Does that sound fair? (pause) What time would be good for you this week?"

Now *that's* creative!

The first time I read that, I belly laughed. Man, that's a quick way to turn that puppy around. If I only had the courage to say that. Just to hear the customer's reaction would be worth the price of admission. I'd already decided that it would not work for me. Obviously, I didn't attempt it. I bumbled my way through that objection doing the best I could for a long time.

Months later, I thought to myself, *"What can I stand to lose by at least trying that line a few times?"* I recorded myself practising it many times and decided to even throw in an innocent chuckle as I started the comeback.

Why didn't I do that sooner?

I was right. It was worth the price of admission just to hear the customer stop dead in his tracks without a further objection. *It worked extremely well.* Only the toughest clients had a negative response. I even had one client ask me how long I'd been a salesperson. He laughed and said that because he didn't have a decent comeback, I'd earned the appointment.

What's the difference?

The first C – *Comfort.* I had no comfort with that statement when I first encountered it. Although it was extremely creative, it was beyond my scope of *courage* at the time. Many of the Professional Salespeople I train have this same reaction to it. *"Dave, I could see you pulling that off, but not me. That's not my personality."*

"Fair enough," I say. *"So adapt it."*

Modify it so that you're comfortable delivering it. *Internalize it and make it yours.* Once you feel at least some level of comfort, you'll be ready to move on to the next C in attempting new sales techniques.

Warning!

 Please keep this mind: You will always feel *some* relative discomfort in trying a new procedure. If you didn't, you'd already be using it. The cliché "No pain, no gain" holds very true. There can be no growth without some discomfort.

The Second C: Courage

No Comfort = No Courage.
Some Comfort = Enough Courage to Attempt the New Method.

 Practise your new technique by recording yourself delivering it, or by standing in front of a mirror to get the full impact. Some salespeople may think this is just plain silly like the common reaction to role-playing.

"Dave, please don't suggest role-playing – I hate it!"

Do professional actors, singers, broadcasters and athletes practise?

Yes. Here's the simple message: if you want to be a Professional Salesperson, you will take your career seriously just like every other performer who wants to increase their skills and abilities. It just takes a bit of *courage*.

Role-playing

Role Playing is not meant to judge you or make you look stupid in front of your colleagues. Find some Professional Salespeople who want to improve. Ask one of the seasoned veterans that you respect on your sales floor to help. Experienced Professional Salespeople are always looking to improve and reaffirm their skill set. There are many different people who would love the opportunity to help out and probably join in, and once you start role-playing you'll actually find it to be *fun and extremely useful*.

Want to *really* improve?

One of the companies I worked for required *video recording* of your presentation in their training program. What you learned when watching yourself in front of the camera was priceless.

"Did I really say that?" "Where did that facial expression come from?" "How many times did I say 'Um?'" "I had no idea I had that nervous habit!" "Geez, I wouldn't buy from me!"

These were all common reactions to the video recording. Do it. It will be one of the best learning experiences of your sales career.

Practise, practise, practise

As I continued to practise, I quickly found that my courage grew as I became more proficient. Suddenly, instead of merely courage, I had . . .

The Third C: Confidence

As Professional Salespeople, we all know that confidence is a job requirement in everything we do. When we become more confident, everything falls into place naturally.

Our nervousness and apprehension are gone, almost as if we want to hear an objection for the opportunity to practise our new skill with grace and style. *"Take your best shot,"* we think. *"I'm ready for it."*

Confidence is a natural by-product of comfort and courage. Through role-playing, you have the venue for the two to occur with confidence closely behind. As your confidence increases, your ability to become even more open-minded grows.

Ever been on a non-qualified call?

The sales industry constantly stresses the need for qualifying customers before you invest much time in them. I agree. More qualified clients lead to more confirmed customers and more sales made. I can also recall, however, many sales calls with clients that I felt didn't have the finances or commitment to engage with me – and they didn't all turn out poorly.

The perfect opportunity

These non-qualified sales calls were the perfect opportunity to try out some of my new techniques in the field. What did I stand to lose? I would rather attempt a new procedure in front of a customer that I felt had a low chance of ordering my product. This way, my role-playing had a venue for field support.

By the time a new technique was attempted on what I felt was a potentially large, qualified client, it was already tried and tested. I had a high degree of confidence with it because of that valuable field experience.

The Fourth C: Change

Comfort + Courage + Confidence = Change.

 Change is inevitable if you proceed through the previous three C's. Skipping one breaks the natural progression and may leave you with the probability of abandoning the new sales technique.

Here are the questions you need to ask yourself:

Did you internalize the new technique and attempt to make it yours?

Did you practise it many times through role-playing?

Did you give it a fair chance before field-testing it?

After carefully observing the Four C's of Learning New Sales Techniques with many salespeople, I now teach them to all of my sales training clients. The Four C's also hold extremely true for different applications such as public speaking and group presentations.

CHAPTER 4
Seven Steps to Your Master's Degree in Organization

Every Professional Salesperson knows that one of the key components to success is organization. Yet many of us struggle with this concept, always looking for ways to become more efficient. *If I wasn't so busy, it would be easier to be more organized!* While many of us have had this thought, the statement itself is ironic. *If you were better organized, maybe you wouldn't be so busy.*

Though there are hundreds of apps available for your smartphone or tablet that promise to make you a more organized salesperson, there are also several tried-and-true "old-school" methods. In this chapter, we'll cover some of these traditional methods before looking at some of the newer technologies.

Step 1 – Organize your workspace

 This seems obvious, yet it's the first necessary step. Let's face it; even organized, structured salespeople have some sloppy habits. So look around you. Does your workplace promote efficiency?

Administration is not the strength of the average Professional Salesperson. If you don't have this skill, ask for advice from someone in your office who does. Detail-oriented people love to help others improve in this area because they take pride in their organizational skills.

Professional Salespeople clean up their workspaces and get organized before even thinking about Step #2.

Step 2 – Put it back

Remember when your mom said, "If you put it back where it belongs, you'll know where it is next time you need it"? Mom was a smart woman. In my case, both my parents drilled that message into me. I was lucky, although at the time I recall feeling much different.

Back to Step 1: Do you have stuff lying around that isn't in its rightful place? Put it back! This simple discipline saves a tonne of wasted time searching for stuff that should be where it belongs.

Step 3 – When something occurs to you, write it down. Now!

No, not when you're driving. (Professional Salespeople have higher insurance premiums for a reason – we tend to do far too much multi-tasking while driving.) Pull over and, when it's safe, write it down.

Recording your ideas is key to being truly organized. *If you write it down, you won't have to remember it.* You know exactly what I mean. If you can remember everything that needs to be done with every one of your clients, you're not working with enough clients!

Step 4 – Diarize follow-ups in your calendar

The last task when contacting a client or co-worker is to record your actions in your follow-up system and/or calendar. What did you do, what actions are required and when is the next date of required action?

Record that date in your calendar! I realize that while most Professional Salespeople will be using a technology-based system these days, perhaps you're a veteran who's using your familiar Day-Timer. My message is the same.

Record the date please. *Do this before another distraction comes along!* Don't allow anyone or anything to hijack your focus.

Follow this system and you won't have to rely on your memory for anything! On the date of follow-up, you will open the file and see what action is required and why it is required.

This step requires discipline that pays off with great rewards as you become an efficient, organized Professional Salesperson that lets nothing slip by.

Step 5 – Plan tomorrow as the last task on your calendar today

That's right. *Make an appointment with yourself from now until the end of the year as the last appointment in your workday.* Every day. This is your 15 minutes of uninterrupted time to specifically plan your day before it starts.

Before the phone rings in the morning, before the hallway conversations, before the client from hell hijacks your day and before your sales manager asks to have a quick conversation with you.

This is a distinguishing quality of the most organized, accomplished people in the world.

If you're planning your day as the first task in the morning, the infamous words of Dr. Phil should ring out. "And how's that workin' for you?" How many times have you decided to start your day with this task to only lose control of what you really wanted to accomplish? Unforeseen circumstances can – and usually do – occur. That's why it makes sense to plan tomorrow as the last task *today*.

The end of day tends to be slower and less frenetic than the morning. Some people have already left the office and your interruption factor is at its lowest. Now is the time to prepare for tomorrow before tomorrow's chaos even starts.

Step 6 – Get a yearly planner

Before the Professional Salespeople who are techies take exception with this, allow me to explain. I'm a technology geek. In my office, I have a Samsung Ultrabook, a PC, a TV for late-breaking news and stock prices, an iPad and an iPhone. I continually have to restrain myself from buying the latest technology toy.

Still, on my wall hangs a huge, low-tech yearly planner on which I record everything my company is doing for the year. Appointments, business travel, holidays and vacation time are all jotted on the yearly planner.

Every day you're busy doing tasks that need to be done to move the revenue needle ahead. It's the proverbial forest through the trees. *When do you get the opportunity to get in a helicopter a thousand feet in the air to see the entire forest – all of your efforts – from that perspective?* A yearly planner shows you what you're doing and how well you're doing it. Your failure to use one just means you'll be kept busy – and not necessarily in a good way.

Your yearly planner will also help you monitor your activity level. Your job is to fill up the blank space with the activities that move your sales ahead. My planner hangs on my wall facing my desk. Every time I walk into the office it calls out to me – *"Get on the phone, make some appointments, and drum up some business!"* In order to do that with one of my tech toys, I'd have to proactively turn the gadget on and open the appropriate file.

Step 7 – Make the best use of technology

 Technology has introduced Professional Salespeople to many wonderful tools. The advances made in the past few years allow you to take your sales career to the next level in a simple, efficient and user-friendly way. I also know, however, that there are a lot of salespeople who aren't entirely comfortable with the latest tech wizardry.

If you're one of them, this next section is primarily for you.

I fought technology for years

The traditional methods worked just fine for me, thank you. I reached great levels of sales and management success without being glued to the latest tech toy on the market. I took pride in my personal relationships with clients and staff members, and in my abilities as a Professional Salesperson.

I told many people that there is no replacement for the face-to-face call and real people skills. There isn't! I was OK letting the rookies walk around with their gadgets bumping into walls and forgetting how to appreciate human interaction. That wasn't for me!

A long time ago

I can recall the day my employer decided that all salespeople were getting PCs at their desk. *Great, how about the company investing in a training program to teach me how to use it?* I still recall someone telling me that my computer was slow because I didn't close any files for the entire first month. I just kept opening new ones. Yep, that was me.

Then I turned 50

When that day came, I realized something. I had made a conscious decision to be closed-minded – something that had never happened before. On that day, I decided I wasn't going to allow myself to become a technology dinosaur and watch the next generation of salespeople pass me by.

Out of my way - I have a plan!

I was going to become the grey-haired, experienced Professional Salesperson who had mastered the best of both worlds. I wanted social media enthusiasts half my age to ask me how I managed to gain all those LinkedIn connections and Twitter followers without paying for them. I'll share my secrets in chapters 36-41. *"Dave,"* they'd say. *"How do you manage to dominate the first five pages of the search results when I type 'Dave Warawa – PROSALESGUY' in Google?"*

Feel – Felt – Found

 If you've been around the sales industry for a few decades, you know the communication technique *Feel – Felt – Found.* Many successful multinational companies have included it in their sales training programs.

"I know how you feel"

I was intimidated by technology and the rapid move to it. It seemed like if you weren't ahead of the game, you were automatically behind. Any Professional Salesperson that wasn't tech-friendly was dated overnight.

"I felt the same way"

Just when I finally got this sales thing figured out, technology came along and made me look archaic and out of touch.

"Here's what I found"

The biggest fear in everything, especially technology, is fear of the unknown. Guess what? It's not so scary once to get to know it! Once you understand some basic concepts and gain a bit of confidence, you'll be on your way to becoming a tech-friendly pro.

Find someone you trust who might be able to assist you. Sign up for a class. Google your questions and instantly find answers – YouTube has a video on virtually anything you want to learn about. Two words: *Reach Out!*

You are not alone

Please understand that there are many experienced Professional Salespeople in your company that feel exactly like you do. Believe it or not, you have the ability within yourself to learn and embrace technology. Just get started and don't let your ego or lack of confidence hold you back. Who cares what people think? Frankly, I think you'll find people have a lot of respect for you in your quest to become tech-savvy.

Technology for the professional salesperson

 Here's my biggest suggestion:

Use one integrated system for everything – all the necessary job functions of a Professional Salesperson. It needs to be fully functional in the office and in the field. *Your technology-based platform needs to be your administration system, task master and communication coordinator.*

Here's the great news

This type of system is available on a handy little device called a smartphone. I'm a personal fan of Apple and have an iPhone and iPad. I also have a Samsung Ultrabook for compatibility reasons with my clients.

Here's what technology allows me to do through the right hardware and apps:

- *Make appointments on my calendar in the office and from the field*

- *Diarize follow-up calls and emails to clients*

- *Create a projects file for clients and internal initiatives*

- *Access email and Internet through WiFi and 4G*

- *Access contact information complete with phone number, email and specific client information*

- *Capture images and record videos for client/internal purposes*

- *Source out great articles on the Internet to send to clients*

- *Electronically share contact information through my own QR Code*

- *Access social media and self-education resources*

- *Read books and listen to Podcasts to stay current and well-informed*

- *Access maps and receive navigation instructions to clients' locations in unfamiliar places*

- *Access calculator, financial planning and tracking tools*

- *Instantly view weather conditions while travelling*

- *Bypass the counter at car rental agencies*

- *Use a built-in alarm clock*

- *Web-conference with clients using Go To Meeting and Face Time*

- *Dictaphone/Voice Memos with email capability when required*

- *Access lifestyle apps to listen to music, relax and unwind*

Observations

I no longer get annoyed waiting for a doctor's appointment. Airline layovers and delays can be my most productive time. *I have a mobile office with all the functionality and capabilities of my actual bricks-and-mortar office.*

Wait!

If buying a tablet, please don't save a few bucks and get the WiFi-only version. You want mobility in all field situations to make the most of your time.

Above all, please embrace technology. It's a wonderful asset and can really enable you to get to the next level in your professional development.

CHAPTER 5

The Five Success Skills of Professional Salespeople

As I mentioned earlier, I've been fortunate enough to sell many different products and services in my professional sales career. They've included training programs, media strategies, real estate and life insurance.

I also benefitted from a great start to my career upon completing broadcasting school many years ago. I was an on-air radio and television broadcaster for many different media outlets. A variety of different opportunities gave me experience in being a personality, newscaster, sportscaster, reporter and live broadcast remote host.

I started in sales, yet didn't realize it

All of these jobs had one common denominator. They involved *the art of persuasion and enticement.* I had to learn how to get people to listen to me. While it doesn't cost anyone a nickel to tune into a TV or radio station, it does take talent to engage the audience and keep them listening. Advertiser dollars depend on it.

How is that any different from sales?

After a few years of media work, I realized that Professional Salespeople seemed to have great incomes. Some of them, incredibly so. Even more than doctors, lawyers and all those professionals society respects a lot more than salespeople. Pushy, persistent peddlers, remember?

It was time to take the plunge.

I'd had enough of living paycheque to paycheque on a fixed (read: "low") income. I was confident I could learn how to be a Professional Salesperson – one that made great money and had pride in the profession.

Here's what I discovered:

Over the course of many different sales positions, I discovered five essential skills that led to success no matter what I sold or for whom I worked. These Five Success Skills not only provided me with a great future, they also allowed me to go home at the end of the day and like the reflection I saw in the mirror. I was truly successful. I wasn't just someone who made great money. I was also someone who was respected by his customers, colleagues and managers.

Not only are these skills great for sales, they're applicable in many professional and personal situations! They're just as effective in the workplace as they are in conversations with friends and family. I later recalled using the same skills in my journalism background as a reporter. They're great life skills because they're all about effectively communicating with people in a manner that they appreciate.

No more misunderstandings!

"Why didn't you say that in the first place?" How many times have you heard or thought that in your dialogue with people? These five skills will wipe that phrase out of your mind.

How do you feel about this?

In the following five chapters, each one dedicated to one of the Five Success Skills, you'll learn to communicate effectively with your customers by finding out *how they feel and why they feel that way.* Sales, when it comes down to it, is about feelings. **People buy based on feelings and justify the purchase based on logic**. Remember that statement. Even the most detailed, formal accountant buys based on feelings. They *feel* like they make the right decision based on facts, figures and logic.

So tell me: *How do you feel about becoming a more successful salesperson?*

CHAPTER 6
Questioning - The First of the Five Success Skills

Stop talking. Just shut up. No one cares what you think. Prospects don't know you. They already have their guard up. The second you start yapping about something with no regard to their needs, you're done. Finished. Kaput.

Professional Salespeople ask great questions

Lose any belief you have that your success is based on being forceful, a talk-a-holic or a great closer. The opposite is true. Your success, and your ability to acquire knowledge and education, is based on your ability to ask great questions. *The person who asks the questions controls the communication and has the opportunity to gain great insight into the perspective of the other party.*

Be authentic & sincere

You're asking questions because you *care* about the answers. After all, you're trying to learn something about the other person. *What makes them feel the way they do?* Did they arrive at their perspective based on personal feelings, previous experiences or opinions from other credible sources? Just remember: no matter what their perspective, they are entitled to their feelings, whether you agree with them or not.

Ask open-ended questions

Open-ended questions are those that don't encourage a short answer. They're designed to open people up to talk about the opinions and emotions that are behind their way of thinking.

For example, instead of asking *"Would you like to have life insurance?"* you might consider asking something like, *"How would your family be financially affected should you die suddenly?"* See the difference?

That question was drilled into me during my time as a door-to-door life insurance salesperson.

By asking thoughtful, open-ended questions, you'll learn about your prospect's decision-making process and what motivates them to do what they do. There's always a motivating reason. Asking the right questions enables you to read their blueprint and predict future reactions to situations and events.

The best open-ended question

Of all the great open-ended questions you could ask, I have a favorite. It starts with four great words.

"Tell me more about (topic)"

This question always elicits a detailed, more meaningful answer. I always experience communications success when asking this question. The person answering opens up and gives valuable insight into a further explanation of what they mean and how they feel.

Try asking this question a few times and watch it become a regular method for you to understand human behavior and what motivates people to act the way they do.

Tact & diplomacy

If you want to be allowed to ask high-level, open-ended questions, you need *trust*. Your prospect isn't going to tell you what she sees as her company's biggest vulnerability unless she fully believes that you are on her side. It's all about the interpretation of your personal agenda – are you helping her for *her* best interests or selling her for *yours*?

Your ability to earn trust will make or break you. Before you blurt out questions that may be perceived as prying, think of how you would react were the question asked of you. In what way could the question be phrased differently in order to encourage your prospect to open up? Though it can be difficult if the two of you have starkly different personalities, the New Golden Rule should be your guide: **Do unto others** *as they would prefer done unto themselves.*

What happens if the customer is making the wrong decision based on misinformation?

There are many ways that people can get the wrong information, and Professional Salespeople deal with this issue very often. When you're confronted with it, fight the urge to respond like this:

"Look, I'm just saying, that's not correct. I know it to be a fact."

"You're wrong" accomplishes nothing even when you're right.

A vacuum cleaner salesperson called one of my friends one day. After doing his demonstration, the salesperson tried to close. My friend said, "No thank-you" after hearing the price, which he felt was simply too high even though it was a great vacuum. Here was the salesperson's reaction:

"So I guess keeping your home clean isn't important to you?"

My friend asked him to leave. Sorry. The "insult close" doesn't win favour, and it certainly doesn't encourage people to buy. He could have responded differently and possibly even salvaged the sale. Imagine if he'd answered instead with a sincere question like:

"So I can get a better understanding of your perspective, could you take a few minutes to tell me where you're coming from?"

If you don't show a true desire to communicate, then don't expect anyone else to go there. Robert Kiyosaki, author of the "Rich Dad, Poor Dad" books has a great quote. He says, *"Communication is not what is said or written – it's what is heard and received."*

Closed-ended questions

It's a common misconception that a closed-ended question is one that elicits a "yes" or "no" response. While this is certainly one type of closed-ended question, other examples include any question that requires a short response of just a few quick words.

"What's your favourite colour?" "When would you like to start?" "Does this make sense?" These are all examples of closed-ended questions.

Closed-ended questions are also important, and Professional Salespeople know the role they play in effective communication. Closed-ended questions provide quick answers to ensure the communication is kept on track.

The one-two punch of effective questioning

Great questioning, then, is a combination of both open-ended and closed-ended questions. You're already doing this in everyday conversation. Concentrate on asking more open-ended questions to gain insight into the other's person opinion, and use closed-ended questions to keep the conversation progressing.

Advanced Questions

Most of us can remember to ask the obvious questions. Becoming adept at asking more advanced questions, though, will greatly help you identify other factors that might influence your customer's purchase decision. When asked sincerely, advanced questions make the customer feel that you care enough to make sure they're making the right decision.

Professional Salespeople always go the extra mile to ensure the buying experience is a positive one based on the customer's desires and needs. Here are a few examples of advanced questions that help them determine what those desires and needs are:

Professional Automotive Salesperson

Basic question: Are you looking for a 4-wheel drive truck?

Advanced Questions: What appeals to you about a more powerful 4-wheel drive truck? How often do you go camping? How long might you keep your current trailer? Might you consider a larger trailer in the future? Who's going to be driving the truck? Will the truck be used for commuting?

Professional Media Salesperson

Basic question (to a business owner): Why do people buy your products and services?

Advanced Questions: What is the top motivator to buy your products versus those of your competitors? Out of 10 people who walk into your store, how many buy? What's the biggest reason people *don't* buy when they come in? Who do you lose the business to? Why might they buy at that business instead of yours? What can you do to change that? What's the first word that comes to mind when people hear your business name?

Ask great questions that make customers stop and think and you'll learn much more than the salesperson who just asks the obvious ones. You'll also make many more sales, and create trusted relationships with repeat customers in the process.

CHAPTER 7
Active Listening - The Second of the Five Success Skills

We've seen the importance of asking great questions – you want to hear the answers to gain a better understanding of the prospect's feelings. Without mastering the skill of active listening, however, that understanding will pass you by.

Feelings are the motivators that cause one person to want to buy and another to continue gathering information. Active listening is an acquired skill that will help you tell the difference (plus much more). All great interview hosts, reporters and psychiatrists are excellent active listeners. So are the truly successful Professional Salespeople.

What active listening is not

Active listening is not waiting for a break in the conversation to make your point, nor is it feigning interest in what the other person is saying while you fumble around in your head for your next great argument. This is one of the most common pitfalls of inexperienced salespeople. They think it's their job to sell you. The more they talk, the more they believe you'll listen. As I hope by now you realize, they're wrong. *The more they talk, they more their prospects tune out.*

There's a difference between hearing, listening and active listening. *Hearing* is the most basic – if you have a pair of ears in good working order, then congratulations – you're hearing.

Listening involves understanding what people are saying based on the *words* they use. Though it's a good start, not everyone is skilled at picking the best words to describe how they really feel. If they were, you wouldn't hear phrases like *"Do you know what I mean?"* and *"I'm probably not explaining this very well."*

Potential buyers need help, support and guidance from a Professional Salesperson to know that they are being clearly understood. The more they get that from you, the more they will share based on the rapport and trust that's being established. You need to make your prospect know that it's perfectly fine to feel the way they do.

What active listening is

Active listening is understanding the *full meaning* of what your customer is saying based on the *words they use* and the *emotions they express*. Here's the equation:

Hearing Words Used + Understanding Emotions Expressed = Active Listening

To fully understand the emotions expressed, Professional Salespeople listen for what's *not* being said. The tone of the customer's voice, the pitch, the inflection on specific words and the pace of their communication are all signals. Body language, movement of their eyes, eyebrows, hands and body, as well as their general posture, can also tell you a great deal about how they're feeling and what they really mean.

When customers are being sincere and open with you, their emotions will back up the words they use. That's a sign that they are genuinely sharing with you. If they aren't, it may be because they aren't feeling comfortable with you. As we've seen, many people have a bad attitude toward salespeople based on previous experience. Continue to be sincere by asking great questions to show you want to help. As you build trust, you will encourage your prospects to share more of their feelings.

A learned skill

It takes much time and practise to become a great active listener. You need to be patient and allow your customers the opportunity to keep talking and expressing themselves. Not only are Professional Salespeople great active listeners, they also show the outward signs of active listening.

In person

Work on showing signs of empathy with a positive, welcoming expression on your face. Nod your head in agreement, even if you don't agree. Remember, you're trying to encourage them to share so that you can learn more about them – *not pass judgement*. You're trying to understand how they think based on how they feel.

On the phone

A patient, quiet and sincere tone with the occasional verbal acknowledgement will go a long way. Though communication is tougher over the phone due to the lack of visual indicators, it's not impossible. Use positive words like *"Yes"* and *"I understand."* Your verbal expressions of support will encourage your customer to continuing talking.

Don't ever do this!

Interrupt. I hear inexperienced salespeople interrupt all the time. Even experienced salespeople will interrupt at times because they wish to make what they feel is a great point. Using the phrase *"Sorry for interrupting, but..."* does not make it OK. It's not only impolite; it's a sure sign that you're not actively listening.

Think of it this way

You ask great questions to hear great answers. Why in the world would you hijack the conversation to get the customer to STOP talking? *Just shut up and listen*! You will get the chance to speak after they've finished talking. They might be about to make a great point and give you a gold nugget of vital information – your interruption might cause that point to be lost as the customer loses momentum in being sincere with you.

Wait for your moment

A great mentor of mine taught me a valuable habit. Whenever you had a conversation with him, he would never interrupt. He would listen to you and nod his head. Occasionally, he would jot down a word or two on a memo pad on his desk. He would wait for you to fully express yourself, and then he would make his points. It would start like this: *"You said something about (topic) a few minutes ago. I had the same challenge years ago. Something that really helped me was (advice)."*

After observing this many times, I asked him what he was writing down. *"Key words,"* he said, *"that help me remember the point I wanted to make. I just wanted you to be able to express yourself fully."*

What a great way to allow people to communicate. It sure beats interrupting!

Fight your emotions

This can be tough, especially if you feel your prospect is wrong based on misinformation. This is where it's important to sharpen your skills at tact and diplomacy. Remember, people feel the way they do based on the information they have. Give them different information diplomatically and they might change their perception. *You will not change it for them.* What you can do is give them great information sincerely that causes them to want to *adjust their own perspective.*

Always allow your customers the opportunity to save face. I have won many people over by telling them that they weren't wrong. They had an opinion based on the information they had. *The better the information, the better the decision.* That statement makes them feel good about themselves and the relationship that they're starting with you.

A great sign

Professional Salespeople know when they're on the right track. Customers will start to relax, share more information and drop their guard. The moment your customer starts asking *you* questions, you know they're engaged in the process.

CHAPTER 8

Paraphrasing - The Third of the Five Success Skills

Of all five Success Skills, this one is the toughest. It's also the most effective.

Paraphrasing is the trademark of a highly skilled, well-trained Professional Salesperson. The world's master communicators paraphrase. They also understand that this art requires hard work and consistent development to turn it into a strength.

Once a Professional Salesperson becomes proficient at paraphrasing, he uses the technique constantly. To this day, in fact, I can't turn it off – whether the conversation is personal or professional, paraphrasing has become so hard-wired into my subconscious that it's become a hallmark of the way I communicate.

Paraphrasing ensures proper communication and accurate understanding of your customer's perspective and is a vital skill to master.

What is paraphrasing?

Paraphrasing is repeating, *in your own words*, what you believe your customer is saying based on their words and feelings. Paraphrasing ensures you have an accurate impression of their true feelings. The first two success skills – questioning and active listening – lead directly into the paraphrase.

Here's the equation:

Great Questions + Active Listening = The Opportunity for Accurate Paraphrasing

Note that it's an opportunity; not a guarantee. You must learn the art of paraphrasing by capturing the true feelings of the customer. Customers may not have the gift of using the perfect words to explain how they feel, so you must learn to become a skilled paraphraser.

Once you've become adept at paraphrasing, you'll be capable of establishing great rapport and trust with your prospects. Professional Salespeople who are great paraphrasers are viewed with respect, which sets them clearly apart from their competitors.

Paraphrasing "trademark phrases"

Professional Salespeople will often start their paraphrase with a variation on one of the following statements:

"If I understand you correctly, you feel that . . ."
"Let's see if I'm on the right track – you would like to . . ."
"Help me make sure I understand you perfectly. You want to . . ."

These phrases tell the customer that the Professional Salesperson wants help to understand their feelings, needs and desires. It's the difference between *selling* to customers vs. *helping* them buy the right product.

Once you become comfortable paraphrasing, you may not have to use these trademark phrases. You might not even ask a question. Based on your skills, you may be able to paraphrase simply by making a statement, rather than asking for clarification.

Capture the emotion

Remember, the point of paraphrasing is to gain clarity on the feelings behind the words. So when you paraphrase, go beyond words and capture that feeling.

Choose the right words that best represent both what the customer is saying *and what you believe she's feeling.* If you weren't actively listening, you will be in big trouble fast.

In one of my sales training sessions I once gave the audience a memorable example of paraphrasing. I asked someone to share the details of their best vacation ever. A mother with young children quickly spoke up:

Mother: *Disneyland!*

Me: *Sounds great, tell me more.*

Mother: *I had never gone there before and my husband and*

	I thought it would be a great place to take our two daughters last summer.
Me:	*How old are the girls?*
Mother:	*Three and five.*
Me:	*What was it like?*
Mother:	*Amazing! It was like a dream come true for them. They were excited and couldn't wait to go. The smiles on their faces every day of the trip were worth every dollar we paid. It was such a great holiday! We'll never forget it.*
Me:	*You must have taken incredible pictures.*
Mother:	*Oh, we did.*
Me:	*So, Mom decided to take her girls on the trip of a lifetime that she never got to take when she was little. No wonder it's your best vacation ever. You must be a great Mom.*
Mother:	*(No response, a little taken back, yet a huge smile on her face.)*

Just listen to people

We all want people to understand us. Showing someone that you do will make a world of difference. The 30-year-old mother's reaction to my final response was based on one key piece of information she said right at the beginning: *"I had never gone there before."*

If I hadn't been actively listening, I would have missed the real gem in her communication. It was her best vacation ever because she gave her girls a gift from her heart. *I'm thinking there were really three little girls on that trip.* We both went away from that 30-second conversation feeling pretty darned good about it.

Signs of great paraphrasing

Professional Salespeople look for signs from customers that show they're on the right track. The words and emotions your prospect expresses after your paraphrase will tell you everything. In my experience, you'll receive either a green light or a red light.

The green light

The customer says "Yes" with conviction and emotion. *"That's absolutely right." "For sure." "Definitely."* Words backed up by positive energy confirm that you've received the green light. Congratulations!

The red light

The customer hesitates, then says something like, *"Not really"* or *"Let me explain."* You'll know when you've hit a red light because the emotions are nowhere near as positive. It's time to put on your active listening hat and . . .

Try again

After your prospect's explanation, apologize and take a second attempt at paraphrasing. Make your best effort to really capture the communication. Trying a third time confirms that you aren't a great active listener. You generally only get two chances for success.

Don't judge

Professional Salespeople understand that great paraphrasing doesn't mean you *agree* with what's being said. It simply means you *understand*. The customer feels good about communicating with you and is impressed by your ability to listen and "get it." People are entitled to feel however they feel – whether right or wrong in your opinion.

Keep trying

Becoming a skilled paraphraser takes much time and effort. Practise consistently with co-workers, friends and family and vary your trademark phrases. With time, it will start feeling natural and you'll get better at it. Eventually, you'll find yourself paraphrasing in daily communication whenever you want to understand someone perfectly. As I said, this skill has sales, business and personal applications.

Find a paraphrasing partner

I suggest this to everyone who wants to become a better Paraphraser. Team up with someone at the office who agrees to partner with you. Every time one of you paraphrases the other, make note of it.

"Nice paraphrase."

Is it corny? Yes. Does it work? Amazingly well in very short time. It reinforces the technique and allows it to quickly become a habit.

CHAPTER 9
Summarizing the Customer's Needs - The Fourth of the Five Success Skills

When a customer's needs are basic and easy to understand, a simple paraphrase will often be enough to capture the communication. With complex buying decisions, however, your questioning will reveal many different needs that will factor into the customer's final choice. Each of those needs has to be addressed and ultimately satisfied.

Professional Salespeople learn to *summarize* each customer's needs at the end of the conversation to show that they understand the full picture of the potential purchase.

A great example of a Professional Automotive Salesperson

 Many years ago, I wanted to buy a 4-wheel drive SUV. There was one model that was of particular interest to me based on appeal, looks and versatility. I walked into a car dealership one day and met a most unassuming Professional Salesperson. My experience with Craig became the basis of a great story that has lasted 25 years.

Craig noticed me looking at the latest model SUV in the showroom and approached me. The following dialogue still holds true today:

Craig:	(nodding as we noticed each other) *It's a beautiful vehicle isn't it?*
Me:	(smiling, looking away) *Yes, it is.*
Craig:	*SUVs are getting a lot of attention these days.*
Me:	*They certainly have a lot of appeal. They don't even look like a truck or a minivan.*
Craig:	*What appeals to you the most about SUVs?*

Me:	*Their looks – exterior and interior. They look classy and are still a 4-wheel drive.*
Craig:	*The 4-wheel drive is important to you?*
Me:	*It is.*
Craig:	*Do you off-road?*
Me:	*No, not at all.* (laugh) *I'm a salesperson and I need reliable transportation in all kinds of weather, especially knowing our winters here in Alberta.*
Craig:	*For sure. Have you ever owned a 4-wheel drive?*
Me:	*Never.*
Craig:	*The traction is amazing. Especially starting and handling on snow and ice. The braking is assisted with ABS. Have you had ABS before?*
Me:	*No.*
Craig:	(explains ABS) *Would you like to have a seat and I can tell you all about this SUV? Would you like a coffee?*
Me:	*Sure, why not?*

I'm now in Craig's office and feeling pretty comfortable with his personality. I chuckle to myself. Wow, he's already got me in his office. *How did that happen?*

Craig:	(returns with coffee) *So, you're in sales* (big smile). *What do you sell?*
Me:	(I proceed to have a five-minute conversation with Craig about my career)
Craig:	*We were talking about the* (*manufacturer make and model*) *SUV. Do you mind if I ask you a few questions?*
Me:	*Sure, of course* (smiling and thinking this guy is a professional – impressive!)

Craig then asks me a series of questions, each of which is designed to open a conversation about a particular selling feature of the vehicle:

Are you married; do you have kids?
(Talk on great interior space, large storage in the back)

How old are they?
(Built-in seat harness information)

How long do you usually keep a vehicle?
(Buy or lease discussion)

Who will be driving it?
(Dual memory seats, visibility and lack of blind spots)

Do you think you'll use the SUV for towing?
(Camping discussion, horsepower, towing capacity)

How many hours are you in the vehicle daily?
(Mileage, warranty, comfort, reliability)

Craig: *OK Dave, thanks for all of that. Let's see if I'm on the right track. You prefer to buy, not lease. Your two boys are four and two. You plan to keep this vehicle for at least three years if not more. You, not your wife, will be driving it mostly, as she has her own car that should be OK for a few more years. You'd like to sell your tent trailer and buy an RV to do more camping. You travel a lot, putting on about 40 miles per day. Did I miss anything?*

Me: (grinning) *No, Craig, you got it all.*

Craig: *Now I'd like to show you the best of this SUV. Do you have time for a test drive?*

Me: *Sure.*

Craig: (walking to a new demo SUV, smiling, excited) *The ride of this SUV is amazing. You'd swear you're in a luxury car, yet with independent 4-wheel drive suspension, you also have great handling and safety.*

Craig proceeds to give me one of his trademark test drives. He drives the SUV down the highway, clearly confirming its incredible ride. After five minutes, he asks me to hang on. He turns off the highway and drives through a ditch and a country field. I'm in shock hanging on for dear life.

Me:	*Whoa*! (thinking this man is perhaps one sandwich short of a picnic)
Craig:	(raising his voice) *See, what I mean? Imagine you and your family going down the highway and having no choice but to do this. At least you'll know everyone is safe – Scared as hell, but safe!*

Craig lets me drive the SUV back to the dealership. I'm just happy to be back on the highway.

Me:	*OK Craig, let me ask you this* (thinking now I've got him, he's going to turn into a car salesman now!). *How does this SUV compare to (another manufacturer)?* (I expect the typical sales pitch – blah, blah, blah.)
Craig:	*Have you ever taken (that other SUV) for a test drive?*
Me:	*No, I haven't.*
Craig:	*Instead of me telling you about it, you should find out for yourself. Do you think you'll be able to take the other SUV for a test drive this weekend?*
Me:	(smiling – Craig doesn't miss a beat!) *I probably can.*
Craig:	*Great, how about I call you Monday and see what you think?*

Craig called Monday. I was in his office Tuesday to buy the SUV.

Did Craig ask great questions? Yes, close to 20.

Was he actively listening? At all times.

Did Craig paraphrase and summarize my many needs? Like a Professional Salesperson.

Was Craig successful? He was selling cars as a summer job while attending university. He became the dealership's top salesperson and decided to make automotive sales his career. He now owns his own car dealership. He teaches Automotive Salespeople to build a relationship with people that turns them into customers - many times over in their lifetime.

I've told that story many times. Craig is a Sales Superstar, a great mentor and an industry leader. In addition to asking great questions, actively listening, paraphrasing and summarizing my needs, he also nailed the Fifth Success Skill for Professional Salespeople.

CHAPTER 10
Personality Projection - The Fifth of the Five Success Skills

Though you may master the first four Success Skills, it's the fifth one that truly makes the experience of interacting with you memorable – memorable enough to make the purchase decision an easy one.

Mastering the other four Success Skills with zero personality is useless. People buy from those they like and trust – it's what makes us human. To be liked and trusted requires, among other things, warmth and caring.

"He's a great guy"

For years, unskilled salespeople having been winning customers over because of their personality. This is not to imply that they're doing anything wrong. Some salespeople suffer from the most common mistakes covered in Chapter 2, yet still seem to have the ability to convince customers to purchase. How? *Personality.*

"I like him."

"She's the kind of person you'd like to give your business to."

These salespeople can be relatively successful even with some specific shortcomings. Should they lack proper follow-up, detail orientation or even competitor knowledge, they make up for it with their sincerity, smile and eagerness to please. Yet why not add strong learned skills to your great personality for a bigger customer impact?

Think of it this way . . .

Which of these salespeople has a better chance of getting your business?

Stone Cold Steve, who is concise and nails the first four Success Skills without crackling a smile?

or

Bumbling Barry, who has a sincere, approachable personality, yet no ability to address your needs?

Or, would you buy from *Right On Rebecca*?

Right on Rebecca is the ultimate professional. She asks great questions based on her sincerity to help and actively listens to what you're saying. She educates you and earns your trust while never pushing you. Rather, she creates a sense of urgency within you to *want to* buy.

Rebecca has a warm personality and is enthusiastic and eager to help, yet she doesn't go overboard and make you want to run for cover. You feel she *deserves* your business because she treats you with respect, knows her stuff and genuinely has your best interest at heart. You want to see her successful, and so you decide to buy from her. You're so impressed, in fact, that you tell your friends and family to go see her when looking for her product.

Get the message?

It's the combination of using *all Five Success Skills* together that makes you a Professional Salesperson. The first four skills are the steak. The fifth is the spice and sauce. Don't make the mistake of choosing one at the expense of the others – no one wants a dry, tasteless steak, a handful of spices or a bowl of sauce. Put them together, though, and who can resist?

CHAPTER 11
The Many Skills of Professional Salespeople

There are many skills required to be a Professional Salesperson. Grab a pen and paper and start listing the ones that you believe are important. You'll likely find yourself struggling after 10 or 15, yet there is easily three times that many.

Below is an alphabetical list of the key attributes of successful Professional Salespeople. As you browse them, ask yourself: *"How many of these do I have? Which ones could I use some work on?"*

Ambitious	Enthusiastic	Organized
Adaptable	Ethical	Passionate
Active listener	Focused	Patient
Asks questions	Flexible	Persistent
Avid reader	Gifted	Positive
Believes in the product	Good with people	Practical
Committed	Good humoured	Prompt
Competitive	Good at math	Quick-thinker
Creative	Gregarious	Reliable
Curious	Great writer	Resilient
Confident	Hard-working	Resourceful
Competent	Energetic	Self-disciplined
Conscientious	Honest	Sincere
Convincing	Impatient for results	Social
Detailed	Inquisitive	Tenacious
Diligent	Integrity-based	Tough
Driven	Knowledgeable	Trustworthy
Eager	Likable	Watchful
Educated	Motivated	Well-balanced
Empathetic	No pressure	Willing to risk

Soft Skills?

In many professions, these attributes are considered *soft skills*. In Professional Sales, they are a necessity. While an accountant has to be great with numbers, being good-humoured is not a necessity, though it is a positive attribute. A doctor needs to be competent, yet having a warm personality makes him so much better. Those skills are a job requirement for Professional Salespeople.

Not for Professional Salespeople

Can you afford to be poor at any of these? Which ones? If you aren't detailed and organized, your lack of attention will cost you credibility with your customers and lose potential sales. If you aren't practical, you'll lose touch with clients. If you aren't impatient for results, you will accept responses like *"I'm still looking,"* or *"email me something."* To be a Professional Salesperson, you need to possess virtually every one of these attributes – and you have to be great at many of them.

What If I'm not?

Find a way to get better. Now.

Read. Type your deficiency into Google and help yourself to dozens of blogs designed to help you improve. The information you need is at your fingertips and costs you nothing. Talk to people in your area who possess the attributes you lack and ask for tips. Resources are easily available – you just have to use them.

Can a weakness become a strength?

While this is possible, it takes huge personal willpower and a desire to look within and make the changes required to do so.

Your weaknesses are not something in which you take pride or enjoyment. You've been dealing with them for years and are probably super-sensitive to them. If they are strong weaknesses, you've probably heard about them before from your managers, clients and trusted allies. Your bravest customers may have even pointed them out. Yes, you can turn a weakness into a strength. That shouldn't, however, be your goal.

Manage your weaknesses

Instead, find ways to make your weaknesses manageable. Professional Salespeople will increase their skill level in their sensitive areas to ensure that it's not an issue with their customers or employer. Delegate! I've seen some of the smartest Professional Salespeople hire others to do the tasks they hate.

Think about your administrative tasks, for example. I have yet to see a Professional Salesperson who enjoys paperwork. Most of us hate it, yet we understand that it needs to be done. Make a diligent student happy with a part-time income, use the expense against your commissions for the year and focus on something more productive.

CHAPTER 12
The Nine Necessary Attributes of all Professional Salespeople

As we've seen, there are many skills and attributes that make Professional Salespeople great at what they do. There are nine, though, that are *absolute requirements*. These nine attributes are based on what I've learned over more than 30 years of sales experience, both on the street and in management observing hundreds of salespeople. If you are weak in any one of these attributes, *you may not achieve the success you so desire.*

1. Ambition

Lazy salespeople are not successful. Unless you have very strong personal aspirations to succeed, it's not going to happen for you. Success doesn't go around looking for people. You need to seek it. A very successful life insurance salesperson once told me, *"There's a big bag of money waiting for you out there. You just have to go pick it up."*

Do you have the ambition to pick up your big bag of money?

2. Motivation

Motivation, closely related to ambition, is in fact only applicable to those Professional Salespeople who *have* ambition. If you're ambitious and motivated, you're moving in the right direction. Now answer this: *"At what speed are you travelling?"* That is your measure of motivation.

3. Confidence

Sales is not for the weak or timid. You need to believe in yourself and your product. You have to be able to look people in the eye, listen to their needs and put together a convincing proposition to make them want to buy. While product knowledge can be learned, personal confidence is harder to teach. It is, however, a necessity.

4. Integrity

Focus on your customer's needs at all times. Professional Salespeople never recommend a product or service that they wouldn't buy themselves based on similar need. Your personal integrity goes beyond the best interests of your employer's. Your customer comes first; your company second; you third. Keep those priorities straight and you will always have customers and a career as a Professional Salesperson. If you're not currently working with an employer who understands that, find a new employer.

5. Respect and Likeability

When was the last time you bought something from someone who you disliked or had no respect for? If customers don't like you, they won't give you their business. Period.

People will go to great measures and inconvenience themselves to find someone they admire so they can buy from them. Customers who don't like you will take all the great information you provided and make the sale easy for the first likeable salesperson who sells a similar product or service. You do the work. Another salesperson makes the sale.

Perhaps the first lesson of sales should be this: *Don't be a jerk.* Don't give people a reason not to buy from you.

6. Passion

Every successful Professional Salesperson has buckets of passion! You need to love what you do and believe wholeheartedly in what you sell. Passion gets you out of bed in the morning and puts a smile on your face that transfers to your customers. They are swept up in your belief, enthusiasm and positive energy.

Passion is the fuel that makes the fire burn bright.

7. Persistence

Remember the word "No" and what it stands for?

I'm not interested in what you have to offer at this given point in time.

Persistence enables Professional Salespeople to make the most of the essential role of timing in the sales process. Tactful and diplomatic persistence pays off.

A Professional Salesperson who wanted me to hire him many years ago demonstrated the best example of persistence I've ever seen. I interviewed Brent and told him he would be a great addition to our media sales team. Unfortunately, I had no position to offer him at the time. He called me after every holiday weekend to touch base. I told him nothing had changed since we last talked. There was still no job opportunity.

"I know," Brent said with confidence. *"If there was one, you would have called me. I was just wondering how your weekend was. What did you do?"*

I laughed every time. Finally I asked him, *"You don't give up easily, do you?"*

"Nope," he said with a chuckle.

This Professional Salesperson called me for *two solid years.* What could I do? Not hire him? If he was that persistent and creative in getting a job, what would he be like in building relationships with buyers to make a sale? As soon as a position opened up, Brent was hired. This individual would never sell a media campaign to a new client unless they had a solid three-month strategy in place. He needed his clients to get results.

If the business owner didn't have the funds together in the first month, Brent would not take the business. He would tell them to keep setting aside the finances until they could do it right, and he'd call them every month to check on their progress. Sound familiar?

His clients had great success and his new business development was high. Brent built strong, long-lasting relationships with business owners before they even purchased. Later in his career, this Professional Salesperson became a sales manager. Persistence, and an understanding and acceptance of delayed gratification, had made him a Sales Superstar.

8. Work Ethic

Without a strong work ethic, any success you have will be short-lived. *Professional Salespeople work hard.* They have to build relationships with many people, dedicate the time to understand their needs, desires and feelings and treat each customer with a positive attitude.

An intense work ethic is a principle of sales success. Easy sales are rare. For every one that occurs, many other potential sales slip away for reasons beyond the control of the Professional Salesperson. That's after working long and hard doing everything within your power to convince someone to buy.

The cornerstones of success

Together, the preceding eight attributes are the cornerstones of success. You need each and every one of them, in no small amount, to become accomplished in the sales industry. Without the ninth necessary attribute, though, they hardly matter. So what's this ninth, *most necessary* attribute of Professional Salespeople?

9. Drive

How bad do you *want it* versus how bad do you *need it*? Drive is the internal engine that pushes Professional Salespeople. It doesn't make them pushy; it makes them bear down and do what needs to be done over the long term.

*Drive is the practical application of **Ambition**.*

*It gives you the **Confidence** to believe in yourself.*

*Drive requires **Integrity** for those who want to like the person they see in the mirror.*

*It pushes you to earn **Respect** while being **Likeable** to receive the support of your customers and co-workers.*

*Drive reinforces your **Motivation**.*

*It's fueled by **Passion**, enables **Persistence** and is apparent in **Work Ethic**.*

Drive is the power that determines the height and speed of your sales success.

Take away drive and the other eight necessary attributes have no self-sustaining energy. That's why it's the most necessary attribute of Professional Salespeople.

CHAPTER 13

The One Common Attribute of All Sales Superstars

We've listed the 40 attributes of Professional Salespeople and covered in more detail the nine most necessary. What attribute could be left to discuss? Only the one that is common to all Sales Superstars.

First of all, for those of you who may have been wondering, let me explain one thing:

What is a Sales Superstar?

The designation of *Sales Superstar* is a level beyond Professional Salesperson. It's like having a Master's degree in sales. Sales Superstars prove their stardom year after year, no matter what obstacles are thrown in their way.

Their attitude

Sales Superstars do not wish to recognize hardships as excuses for failure. They attain their goals and *then* acknowledge the obstacles that were in their path. It's their *perspective* and *attitude* that makes them different. They don't belong to the coffee club and moan about their challenges to their co-workers. They understand the true meaning of the cliché "misery loves company." They socialize with positive-minded people only and, because of this, may not be the most popular people on the sales floor.

They are fiercely competitive in one of two ways

They either need to be the top Professional Salesperson in their division or they need to be consistently beating their results from the previous year.

They are the top earners in the company and make incredible commissions.

Their annual incomes exceed many doctors, lawyers and those with actual Master's degrees. They dare not tell their neighbours or family about what they earn for fear of jealousy and alienation.

A different twist

Someone once said to me, *"If I had all of your money, I'd burn mine."* I laughed and said, *"Really? If I had all of your money, I'd keep it."* The expression on their face confirmed their unfortunate jealousy and opinion of me.

I had another interesting exchange one time with someone who was educated, sophisticated and salaried. Here's the gist:

Salaried person:	*"I don't understand how my company can pay over $150,000 per year to our top salespeople. How can that person be worth three times what I make?"*
Me:	*"If you owned a company, would you pay a salesperson 15% commission with no salary? This means if they sell nothing, they make nothing."*
Salaried person:	*"Sure, why not? What risk is there in that?"*
Me:	*"What would happen if they brought in over $1,000,000 in annual sales? What would they have earned?"*

It's interesting how that simple spin can change one's perception.

Sales Superstars should make no apologies for the income they take home. They should be proud. After all, they possess most of the 40 Attributes of Professional Salespeople, they have all of the nine necessary ones, and each and every single one of them has an abundance of one final attribute.

 Self-discipline

Self-discipline is the ability of a Professional Salesperson

to function like a business within the structure of the company they represent.

You have customers who buy your product or service from you. While they understand you work for your company, their relationship is with you directly. They buy from *you*. To them, your sales manager and any other company representatives come second. If your customer isn't happy, you'll be first to know.

Remember James, the sales superstar I mentioned back in Chapter 2, the one who had the exceedingly successful year yet couldn't quite put his finger on why? Let me remind you what his response was:

"I don't know Dave. I came to work every day, got on the phone to make appointments, did a complete needs analysis, put together a strategy based on their needs and objectives and confirmed the business. I worked hard with my clients throughout the year to make sure I never took them for granted and I always brought forward new ideas. I didn't do anything other than what you trained me to do."

That's self-discipline.

As a sales manager, I had regular meetings every two weeks with all of my salespeople. My meetings with James always ended with a familiar phrase: *"Just keeping doing what you're doing."* Little wonder why.

James had mastered the attribute of self-discipline. I never wondered where he was. If he wasn't in the office, I assumed he was with a client. If he wasn't with a client, he was taking care of a family situation. He worked from his home office on evenings and weekends. He did what it took to get the job done.

I never put James on a CRM (Customer Relations Management) program or a call report. He would have taken it as an insult. He made his numbers. In fact, his overachievement made up for other salespeople's underachievement, which happens to all Professional Salespeople all the time. *He got it.* He earned the privilege of his freedom.

You can see why Sales Superstars are hard to find. Their self-discipline requires a unique way of managing them to ensure they are focused and productive.

What are the signs of Self-Discipline?

So how do you recognize a Professional Salesperson with

the self-discipline to become a Sales Superstar? What does self-discipline look like?

Self-Discipline *is coming to work every day with the drive that is required to succeed.*

Self-Discipline *is not looking for shortcuts.*

Self-Discipline *is being tougher on yourself than anyone else could be.*

Self-Discipline *is having higher standards for yourself than for your employer.*

Self-Discipline *is making your family understand that taking the kids to the dentist means you might be working at home tonight.*

Self-Discipline *is taking responsibility – not laying blame on a bad client, a tough boss, bad luck or a bad economy.*

Self-Discipline *is playing the role of "victor" despite the roadblocks.*

Self-Discipline *is knowing when you're in a sales slump and what you did last time to get out of it.*

Self-Discipline *is understanding how you deal with change makes all the difference.*

Self-Discipline *is letting go of the things you can't control so that you can influence the ones you can.*

Self-Discipline *is investing in yourself and keeping the receipt for tax purposes.*

Self-Discipline *is looking in the mirror and motivating yourself to get the job done.*

Self-Discipline *is appreciating that nothing truly meaningful comes without hard work and sacrifice.*

Sales Superstars have an enormous amount of self-discipline. It's what sets them apart from Professional Salespeople.

CHAPTER 14
What do Professional Salespeople Really Sell?

Be prepared to give your head a shake. This chapter is going to cause you to redefine what you think you sell, or what you think your company sells. It will give you the opportunity to see what you do on a completely different scale. Professional Salespeople will use this information to differentiate themselves from competitors and avoid facing constant price objections. It might even provide you with the opportunity to provide your customers extra value without giving anything away for free.

Here's the question:

What are you *really* selling?

Let's look at a few common products and services that are sold by Professional Salespeople:

Salespeople	What they sell
Automotive salespeople:	Cars, trucks, vehicles
Realtors:	Houses, businesses, land
Life insurance agents:	Life insurance
Investment brokers/advisors:	Stocks, bonds, investments
Dave Warawa	This book, right?

Nothing revolutionary so far, right? Now look at those products again – what does each one *accomplish*? What purpose does it serve?

Before moving forward, let's start with some basic definitions.

Tangible products

Professional Salespeople sell a product or a service. Products are tangibles – things that rely heavily on the five senses of *sound, sight, taste, touch, and smell*. In many cases, a product, such as a new car, will involve many of these senses for a full customer experience. A test-drive, for example, is a situation in which all five senses come into play.

Think about viewing a new house for sale. It needs to look good – great carpet and upgraded underlay gives you the feeling of luxury. Realtors will always tell you that great scents, like the smell of fresh baked cookies, is inviting and makes the house more appealing to buyers. Having some subtle music in the background can also help establish an inviting atmosphere.

Product features and their benefits

 In tangible sales, a great deal of the decision to buy rests with the product features and how they relate to actual *customer benefits*. The benefits of a feature like an automatic car starter, or air conditioning in a home, seem obvious.

Automatic car starters are great in cold winter climates. Once you have one, you will be convinced that this luxury is now a necessity. Yet they're also a great feature in the summer during record hot days, giving you the opportunity of cooling the car before you get in.

Another feature, heated seats, are quite common, yet *air conditioned seats* are becoming a great luxury feature. Cool air is actually sent through the seat, which has an immediate impact on you as if you just stepped inside a walk-in cooler. The benefit? No more sticking to the seat or arriving to an appointment covered in sweat.

Depending on your climate, air conditioning in a house may seem like a frivolous, costly feature. Really? Do you enjoy having it in your car? Would you buy a car without air conditioning? *Do you sleep more hours per day in your house than you spend commuting in your car?* I certainly hope so.

Ask anyone who has the luxury of air conditioning in his or her home. Almost without exception they'll include it on their list of necessities. The benefits include no more hot restless nights, tossing and turning with windows open and fans running.

Professional Salespeople who sell intangibles have to be able to consistently relate product features to their benefits. Never assume that your customer is aware of them. Simply ask the question – *Have you ever had a (product feature) before?* Even with a "Yes" response, go there with them. *So you're fully aware of what it's like to (experience product benefit)?* You need the customer to acknowledge the benefit to add to the full sales experience.

Features are nice. *Benefits* are what customers want to buy.

Intangible services

Many Professional Salespeople sell intangible services. They are specifically designed to meet a particular need or deliver a particular benefit. There may be no test-drive or actual product that you can examine.

Let's consider, for example, the category of life insurance. No one rushes out one day totally pumped about buying life insurance. You'd much rather take a trip to Vegas or buy something close to your heart.

Buying life insurance provides financial protection to your family should you die. I spent a few years selling this product door-to-door for a major insurer. Only once did a woman claim that she and her husband were just talking about buying life insurance the night before. When she did, I looked around the front entrance of her house, thinking the guys at the office were pulling a fast one on me.

What do life insurance salespeople sell?

Life insurance. Death protection. The ability for your family to be taken care of in the event of your untimely death. *Peace of mind.* Pretty simple to understand, right?

Not an easy sell

As I'm sure you can imagine, selling anything door-to-door is not easy. It's a character-building experience. Most people don't appreciate you knocking on their door, trying to sell them something they think they don't need. "*I have life insurance protection at work through my benefits package*" was a very standard answer the second I introduced myself.

Here was my strategy: I would ring the door bell and really hope that their barking dog would spare my life. I would introduce myself and tell them I was their local life insurance representative. After getting the you-poor-idiot-you-should-have-gone-to-school look, I began asking questions:

First Question:

"Do you mind me asking, do you have a mortgage?"

Virtually everyone said "Yes," with a look of just-go-away-now-please. Admittedly, some people slammed the door in my face and said *"That's none of your business"* or something decidedly less polite. *"Thank-you,"* I'd reply, and I'd move on to the next house. *"Too bad you didn't give me a chance,"* I'd think.

If they didn't slam the door in my face, I'd continue.

Second Question

"By chance did the bank sell you life insurance with the mortgage?"

"Yeah, of course," they'd answer. *"Why?"*

Third Question

"Were you aware that the premium payments go up every time you renew the mortgage?"

"What do you mean?" they'd say.

My opening statement

"The bank sells you life insurance for the term of the mortgage. When you renew the term, you pay a higher premium based on being older. If you have a 25-year mortgage with five-year terms, your life insurance rates will go up each time you renew. Most people don't know that."

"Gee," they would say, *"I didn't realize that."*

"Would you like me to explain that further? If you buy life insurance associated with your fixed-term mortgage, your insurability ends upon the completion of that term. You then renew your mortgage and pay a higher rate based on being that much older. The older you get, the higher

the monthly premium. If you have a 20-year amortization and decide to renew every five years, you'll experience five major premium increases before you pay off your mortgage. The bank is collecting your premium payments and forwarding them to the insurance company based on their mutual business relationship. Now here's the real kicker: the beneficiary is the bank and your mortgage is paid out, eliminating that burden to your bereaved family."

An option that makes sense

I would tell people to consider taking a life insurance policy for the entire amortization period of 25 or 30 years. Right now. They would never have to prove insurability if they became ill and their premiums would be based on their current age and never go up for as long as they held a mortgage. Better yet, the beneficiary would be whomever they chose, whether it be their estate, spouse or a family member.

"Why not take a personal life insurance policy for all of your debt, plus more so that those left behind don't experience any financial hardship from your passing?"

Do you think I managed to get a few people to book appointments with me by giving them this insight? You bet I did. *The moment I related the product feature of individual life insurance to the benefits listed above, people looked at me in a different light.* No one, including their banker, had told them that before.

As a life insurance salesperson, my true product was *knowledge* and *advice* in such matters. My customers bought life insurance because I gave them a compelling reason to do so.

By the way, if you're wondering if this scenario holds true to this day, call your local banker and life insurance salesperson. See what they tell you.

What do Realtors sell?

Homes, businesses and land, right? You want to sell your property and don't want to even think about doing it by yourself, so you call a Realtor. Smart buyers know the advantages of working with their own Realtor when looking to purchase a home.

The Smart Realtors

How many times will you buy or sell a home in your lifetime? Wouldn't it make sense to find a Realtor who is really successful in getting you the *best price as quickly as possible* when you sell? How about the *best price on the best house* when you buy? Wouldn't it be nice to use the same trusted Realtor every time you need one?

Smart Realtors don't sell homes. They sell their expert services as professional marketers, evaluators, negotiators and personal housing representatives over the duration of your lifetime.

So, let's review.

What do these Professional Salespeople sell?

Automotive Salespeople

Professional Automotive Salespeople sell their ability to match you with the best vehicle based on your needs, desires, lifestyle orientation and budget. They attempt to make the transition from your current vehicle to your new one as painless as possible. They try to negotiate the best cash difference from your trade-in vehicle.

If they do this well, and periodically call you to retain their relationship with you, they will probably win your business repeatedly because you feel that they really care and respect you and your business. You will buy many vehicles in your lifetime. Professional Automotive Salespeople want to establish a permanent relationship with you for that reason.

Life insurance agents / investment advisors

These Professional Salespeople provide the opportunity to make wise financial decisions that make and/or save you money in the long term. The insurance protection coverage on your mortgage is just one example.

While buying a 100-year life insurance policy for your child at the age of six might seem strange, for example, a Professional Life Insurance Salesperson can explain that the premiums will be ridiculously low, your child will never have to prove insurability and the beneficiary can always be changed to your child's family if they marry and have children. Information. Education. *Value*.

Realtors

Realtors sell their expertise in showing you solid market research to determine the listing and selling price of your home based on its market value and location. The key is to price your home properly based on market conditions so as to solicit viewings. Viewings will reveal the market's perception of your home and what you are dealing with competitively.

Realtors provide these valuable services to buyers free of charge, as they split the selling commission with the listing Realtor of the house you buy. They represent your interests solely and negotiate for you on your behalf. Since you are going to be buying and selling several homes over your lifetime, find a great Realtor that looks to establish a permanent relationship.

Dave Warawa

 I provide Professional Salespeople with the resources to self-educate, become skilled and devise a proactive plan to engineer their own success. I provide the expertise to apply proven principles of sales success in a practical way that makes sense for you as an individual. None of this material came from formal education. My track record is based on my MBA from the Street.

I wish to give Professional Salespeople the opportunity to feel pride in their profession based on the respect they receive from their clients, co-workers and employers. You can love what you do, like who you are and have a rewarding, lifetime career as a Professional Salesperson. That's what I'm selling.

What do *you* sell?

Figure it out, write it down and live by it. Let it guide your thoughts, words and actions. Look beyond the obvious and consistently over-deliver. Do the little things for customers that make all the difference.

A company I was with once hosted a cruise to entertain our largest customers to show our appreciation for their business. One of my toughest clients was on that cruise with his wife. This guy was a tough person to please, and he had his reasons. He was very demanding and was rarely satisfied unless you did everything perfectly.

As typical of many cruises, a huge display featured all the great professional pictures taken at the main show on the final night. I spotted a glossy 8 x 10 of my client and his wife. It was a great shot and really showed them enjoying themselves. I couldn't resist the urge. I bought it and asked the concierge for a large envelope and piece of letterhead. I wrote a personal note and signed it – *"Thought you might like this"* – and slid it under his door.

I will never forget that experience. The impact that photo made on him was far more than I expected. The respect he had for me from that day forward was far different. All because of something that took so little time, expense and effort on my part. What it taught me was this:

The real product that you have to offer is the experience of dealing with you.

CHAPTER 15

Customers Don't Want the Lowest Price - They Want the Best Value

We live in a world that's obsessed with price. All customers, it seems, want the lowest possible price for the top-of-the-line quality and the best service – and companies largely oblige this fantasy.

Commercials scream this commitment. Retailers boast that they do it better than anyone else. Some go so far is to *guarantee* the lowest price, and price-match or beat any other advertised price by 10 or 15%.

Their strategy is to get you to simply buy from them and not shop around. After all, what business would want to consistently reduce their price because a competitor is advertised lower? At least, that's the marketing strategy designed to entice you.

"I need your lowest price"

Here are some of the most common price objections that are designed to coax Professional Salespeople into lowering their price in fear of losing a potential sale:

"You'd better sharpen your pencil if you want my business."

"We're ready to make a final decision on whom to buy from and we thought we'd give you the opportunity. There won't be a chance for a second round of negotiations so you'd better come in at your lowest price right from the start."

"I can appreciate you would like to get a better price than what I'm offering. If you honestly think you can, I understand. You won't hurt my feelings if you say no. I need to make a quick decision and here's my best offer. Just say yes or no."

Ever heard any of those?

Every Professional Salesperson I know could add a personal favourite to that list. In a later chapter, we'll discuss the art of negotiation, at which point you'll be given the tools to become an expert and actually enjoy the process. For now, let's focus on the relationship between price and value.

Price is what you pay for a product or service.

Value is what you get when you buy a product or service.

Which is really the focus?

While our customers lead us to believe that price is the governing factor in the decision to buy, it's not. Here's why, for precisely the reason I mentioned in chapter 2:

When was the last time you heard someone bragging about the great deal they got on a piece on junk?

Never!

 There is no such thing as a great deal on a piece of junk; no matter what you paid, you paid too much. Junk is worthless. Buying it is embarrassing and is something you don't want to admit to. Ever buy the real cheap version of a product with an extremely low price only to have it break down the next day?

What do you do then?

Shake your head, mutter under your breath and rush out to buy the quality product at a much higher price. We do it so fast, as if we're trying to erase the memory of ever making that wrong purchase.

Which product was more expensive?

The cheap one that broke. You got absolutely nothing out of it other than a lesson in you-get-what-you-pay-for. Consider the combined price of the two products you purchased. That will make you think twice about the next too-good-to-be-true deal.

What we all want is *value*

We want great quality for a fair price. That's what your potential customer is really saying. Everyone wants a great deal. That's bragging rights. The better the product, the greater the story becomes. Of course price is a factor, though *only once quality has been established.* That's based on individual perception, which is something we can change. That's the difference between order-taking and Professional Sales.

When price exceeds value

When price exceeds value, we feel the product is too expensive and we don't buy. We feel it's not worth the price. *Too expensive compared to what?* This is the question to ask your prospect when you're faced with this objection.

Never assume the answer is *"Too Expensive for what I want to pay."* You can chuckle and say, *"I agree, we'd all like to pay less than what we have to."* Then smile and shut up. *Please don't drop your price.* Professional Salespeople are not fish to take the bait. They want the customer to explain their feelings.

You: *"Do you mind me asking why you think it's too expensive?"*

Prospect: *"It's too expensive compared to what I think it's worth;"* or *"Another product down the street is priced lower;"* or *"It just seems like a lot of money."*

Now we're getting somewhere.

When value exceeds price

When value exceeds price, we're satisfied that we're getting a good deal. *Good value for the dollar,* or *bang for the buck,* is what we think. We make the purchase feeling confident that we made an intelligent decision based on the facts and details available to us.

Budget restrictions

Professional Salespeople are aware that no matter how much value exceeds price, we need to be able to *afford* the product. There are limits to what we'll pay for a product or service based on budgeting, access to financing and lifestyle. Many of us would love to own a Ferrari, for example, yet even a blowout sale of just $100,000 for one of those sporty beasts wouldn't necessarily put it within our reach. Practicality and affordability are always factors in the relationship between price and value.

Your options

If price is higher than the perceived value of the product or service you're selling, you really have only two options at your disposal in order to convince the customer to buy:

1. Reduce your Price

Unfortunately, this is where many salespeople immediately go - fast. Reduce the price to get the business. In their defence, many companies allow them to. *What choice do we have if the competition is selling the same product for less?* Good question, and it will be answered shortly.

Stop doing this:

Stop advertising and telling customers that you offer the lowest possible price, the best quality products and that you back it up with the best service in the industry. This claim is one of two things:

A lie

No wonder your customers don't trust you. You're making claims that are untrue, unreasonable and ridiculous. Your customers know better. How can you offer the best of everything with the lowest price of anyone? This is why we, as a society, mistrust salespeople and advertising. Your customers aren't idiots.

The truth

What if you're working for a company that actually does give the best of everything for the lowest price of anyone? Keep your resume current, because this is a formula for bankruptcy.

There's no reason why you should have to always lower your prices to get business.

A note on loyalty

Believe that your loyal customers *want you* to make a profit to stay in business. If they have an established buying relationship with you, they would like to be able to buy from you in the future. If they like and respect you as a Professional Salesperson, they would like to see you do well.

2. Increase Value

A better option than reducing your price is to *add value*. We've already determined that value is based on individual perception. That perception can be changed in the mind of the customer. If we increase value, we can hold price steady and complete the sale. Many Professional Salespeople have heard the term "value-added." The question is, "How do I increase value with *credibility?*"

In many cases, customers are not comparing products and services to the best of their ability. Though the web has greatly increased the sophistication level of the average buyer, they still need the advice and assistance of a trusted Professional Salesperson to guide them in making the right purchase based on their needs. This is the first step in establishing value.

Safety, security and peace of mind

These are strong emotions that we all want to experience as buyers.

Insurance and warranty programs are intangibles that you hope to never use yet appreciate having. One of the best Professional Life Insurance Salespeople I've ever met told me a story that has stuck with me for 25 years.

Years ago, the sales agent who sold the policy was the one who also delivered the insurance payout to the beneficiary when the policyholder died. He said that until you do that, you have no idea the *value* of what you're selling or the impact it makes on people's lives. I still get goose bumps when I think about that.

Value-add products

As a Professional Salesperson, can you (and your company) get creative? Is it possible to offer well-perceived value-added products at no additional cost to the customer? Can these products have great perceived value with low cost to the company you represent? The following are some examples; if they don't apply to you, think of what you might do in your business category for the same impact:

- *The purchase of a cell phone comes with a screen protector or protective case.*

- *During holiday seasons, the customer receives a gift with purchase.*

- *The purchase of computer equipment comes with a memory stick.*

- *Sign up for three years of Internet service and get a free TV (Wow!)*

Value-add services

Adding value-add *services* to increase the perception of value can be even more practical than adding products, as most services have a great profit margin with little to no hard cost. Again, think of an application in your industry, such as:

- *The purchase of a complete set of winter tires includes storage of your alternate tires for the year.*

- *A car dealership includes free service and maintenance of your new car for the first year.*

- *A hot tub company allows its customers no-charge water testing and will email the results to you.*

- *A Realtor provides clients with free use of his moving trailer for local moves.*

In each of these examples, the added service increases the *value perception* in the mind of the customer. Professional Salespeople can really go the extra mile by negotiating with their employer to allow the customer to continue to have these services past the initial purchase period.

You can be an important value-add

Professional Salespeople know that their work ethic, skill, integrity and sincerity have definite value. So is it rude to actually bring it up? Not with a smile on your face! If you're prepared to work harder than your competition before and after the sale, why shouldn't that be a factor in establishing value?

Value is the answer

Professional Salespeople understand the importance of establishing a strong value perception in the mind of a customer. Doing this at great length *before* discussing price can result in no price objection whatsoever. At the very least, it takes the focus off price, making those objections much easier to deal with.

CHAPTER 16
Upsetting the Buyer's Complacency

Professional Salespeople are always looking for ways to motivate people to take action. Without a decision, nothing can occur.

Remember that an objection shows the customer's involvement in the dialogue. Objections can easily lead to buying decisions when enough credible information is presented to change opinion.

Nothing is more difficult to handle in the sales process than someone who is not prepared to share his or her opinion. You must *upset the customer's complacency* in order for a buying decision to be made.

Upset the buyer's complacency

 This was a famous phrase drilled into me during my life insurance training. Let's admit it – no one really wants to buy life insurance. There are many more exciting things to purchase, as there are in the case of similar categories like health coverage, tires, investments and other non-sexy necessities.

In chapter six, we covered the importance of asking great questions. Through active listening, Professional Salespeople can determine who is the complacent customer who's just shopping at this particular stage.

The let-me-think-about-it objection

While the idea of evaluating all the information to make the best decision makes sense, consider this: very seldom does someone go against their gut feeling. This was always my response to "Let me think about it":

"If you don't mind me asking, what is it specifically that you need to think about?"

I would say this with as much sincerity as I could express. Professional Salespeople need to know the reasons why customers are or are not prepared to buy. That allows them to confirm the sale and solidify it. If dealt with properly, objections can lead to a purchase.

Deliver the phrase above without sincerity, and you will be dubbed as just another pushy salesperson trying to close a deal.

What happens then?

Apologize, and say this:

"I'm sorry, that didn't come out right. I'm just trying to find out what I can do to help you make the best decision. The better the information you give me, the more I can help you – does that sound fair?"

Educate the buyer on their objection

Professional Salespeople don't make customers feel bad for having an objection. Always remember, if clients don't like and trust you, they won't buy from you. *Don't be a jerk.* It can be shocking to see how many inexperienced salespeople make this mistake. Acknowledge how the customer feels and provide validity to what they're saying.

"I understand. You're not the only person who feels that way. Here's something to consider…"

What if the customer still wants to think about it?

Great! They are allowed, you know. Many of us like to trust our gut feeling, yet still sleep on it overnight. Any more effort at this point and you run the risk of ruining the rapport and trust that you've worked so hard to build.

If it's a great decision now, it will still be one in the morning.

I've had customers look me in the eye and say that to me. I always give the same response, again with a sincere smile on my face:

"Of course – I understand. Many people feel exactly the same way. Would it be too quick to call you in the afternoon to answer any further questions you might have? Have I answered all of your questions properly? Do you have any more?"

Professional Salespeople need to be assertive, yet not aggressive. No one likes a pushy salesperson, yet customers expect that your confidence and conviction in your product will cause you to gently nudge a potential sale along. You need to know whether your client is being truly sincere about needing more time to think or just being polite by not saying "No." Professional Salespeople have a saying: "It's not the No's that kill you. It's the Maybe's."

Don't give your sale away!

You've worked hard to educate your customer, asked great questions and answered many in return. You've done your best to show the true value in your offer. You believe that you're representing your client's best interests. Don't stop one step away from completing your job – assume and ask for the sale! Get your customer to make a decision one way or the other. If you don't, they may very well give the next salesperson an easy sale based on your hard work.

CHAPTER 17
Sales Inertia and the Three Levels of Activity

 This chapter is going to make every sales manager smile and every salesperson groan. No matter what side of the desk you're on, you will eventually come to an agreement on this issue.

 Every sales manager has had the responsibility of discussing activity levels with their salespeople. Even Professional Salespeople have periods when their activity levels are low, eventually effecting sales results.

As a sales trainer and consultant, it's my job to bring simplicity to complex issues. While grey is a difficult color to explain, black and white are very straightforward.

Sales inertia

Inertia is a term you may recall from physics class back in grade school. It's essentially defined as the tendency of an object at rest to stay at rest and the tendency of an object in motion to stay in motion. If a train is motionless, for example, it will remain that way unless some external force is applied to move it. If the train is cruising along its track at a high speed, it's inclined to continue at that speed until brakes are applied or the external force of friction against the rail slows it down.

Professional Salespeople know intuitively the tremendous force of sales inertia. Have you ever said this before?

"I'm on fire! Every time the phone rings, I make a sale – it's unbelievable!"

or

"Man, I couldn't sell a free sandwich at a picnic on a sunny Sunday. What's wrong with me?"

It's sales inertia.

The definition

Sales inertia: The tendency of Professional Salespeople to continue to sell without effort during a selling streak and to continue to struggle despite their efforts during a sales slump.

Sales inertia is a very real thing, though I can almost see your head shaking in disbelief. Weird, isn't it? For the inexperienced salesperson, it makes no sense. Why are there times when sales keep rolling in with little effort and times when the exact opposite is true? Here is the hard reality:

Activity breeds results. Inactivity breeds excuses.

Ever heard this from your sales manager?

"Your sales are on fire! Just keep it up and you're going to have a record year!"

or

"Your sales are suffering because your activity level is too low. If you don't pick up your pace, you're going to miss the quarter and probably the year."

As much as you don't like hearing that last statement, Professional Salespeople know it to be the absolute truth. Knowing and doing something about it are two different things!

Before I tell you how to deal with the challenge of a sales slump, let me explain the *Three Levels of Activity*. I've used this explanation hundreds of times to motivate and empower business owners, decision-makers and Professional Salespeople. It's been one of the most effective ways to get people "fired up" for positive change.

The First Level of Activity - *Inactivity*

 Inactivity means you do nothing about your situation. It's simply the way it is, and nothing is going to change it. Unfortunately, this is a self-fulfilling prophecy. Any attempt at improvement will probably be useless because you're wasting too much energy feeling sorry for yourself. *Waaah! – poor you.* Sorry, I don't feel as sorry for you as you do.

Inactivity wins an Oscar for its portrayal of the role of "victim." Inactivity means you are out of business – order your headstone today.

The Second Level of Activity – *Reactivity*

When you're reactive, you're able to change your behaviour based on your environment. External factors are controlling your actions and you're doing your best to fight the fires. The fewer there are, the better you fare. If your luck would just change and start going your way for once, you're sure you'd get better results.

Every Professional Salesperson will be in the reactivity phase at some point. The smart ones recognize it, deal with the matter and quickly move on. If you're consistently in a reactive place, though, it's very likely that your actions (or inactions) are keeping you there.

The Third Level of Activity – *Proactivity*

 When you're proactive, you accept your accountability and *develop a strategy to bring about change.* You may be in this position because you put yourself here through previous inactivity. You will no longer complain about your clients, the economy, your budgets, the competition or the sales manager who won't give you a break.

You've decided to have higher standards than what your boss or your company expects from you. You have a plan and are committed to it. Your thinking, behaviour and actions follow your new strategy with confidence. You know that results will come with hard work, enthusiasm and personal dedication.

You have decided to pay the role of Victor.

Get in level three and stay there

Once you have made the decision to become proactive, stay there! Getting out of the inactivity level requires the greatest amount of effort with the least measureable results. All Professional Salespeople have been there – the smartest ones only experience it once.

They have distinct memories of what was required to graduate from inactive or reactive and do their best to always *stay* proactive. In the proactivity level, consistent effort keeps you successful. This means having the self-discipline to keep a checklist of practices that maintain your pace and energy level.

Beware!

I've seen this many times. A salesperson makes a conscious decision to do what it takes to be proactive and change her direction. She develops a strategy with a strong action plan, stays focused and committed for a sustained period of time and is rewarded for her efforts. Results follow and she finds herself back on top, feeling confident and with a sense of real accomplishment.

Since the problem is solved, she then decides to stop doing all the things that made her successful and goes back down into the reactive or even inactive level. After all, she deserves a break for her hard work, doesn't she?

Once again, sales inertia sets in and the train comes to rest. Within a few weeks or months, the pattern returns and another sales slump sets in. What happened?

Consistency

Professional Salespeople treat their employment like a business that constantly needs to be maintained. It's no different than going to the gym – all of your hard work and great results go by the wayside if you stop moving ahead for a few weeks.

Find out what it personally takes for you to get into the proactive level. Once you're there, determine exactly what it takes to stay there. That's what Sales Superstars do.

CHAPTER 18
Everything before the Word "BUT" is BS

In chapter 14, I gave the following example of acknowledging a customer's objection to buying:

"I understand. You're not the only person who feels that way. Here's something to consider..."

Now let's insert one common word that we use on a consistent basis and see what happens:

*"I understand. You're not the only person who feels that way. **BUT,** here's something to consider..."*

Everything before *BUT* feels like BS

One small word can change the entire meaning of your message. *BUT* is negative and condemning. It makes the statement before it seem insincere and patronizing. It makes the person you're communicating with feel like you're agreeing with them one second and then disagreeing the next. Just look at the impact made using *BUT* in the following statements.:

"I can appreciate how you feel, but if you consider the value of our product over the competition..."

"I know you were really looking at delivery before the weekend, but we're short staffed..."

"I understand that you'd like to pay a lower price, but consider the options on this model..."

What the customer hears:

"I don't appreciate how you feel. Let me set you straight..."

"I don't care about your desire at have delivery before the

weekend. It's not possible."

"Stop being cheap. You get what you pay for, OK? If you want the upgraded model, pay the price for it."

This will be very tough

You've been using the word *BUT* for a very long time. It will seem like an impossible task to remove it from your dialogue. You'll catch yourself using the word, then suddenly stop, thinking *"Dang, I did it again!"* Stopping mid-sentence will actually draw attention to the *BUT* and make it worse temporarily, but it's also a sign that you're getting close to banishing it completely.

So how *should* you say it?

Professional Salespeople pause after the first statement. They surgically remove the word *BUT* and start the next statement.

"I can appreciate how you feel. (Pause) Consider the value of our product over the competition..."

"I know you were really looking at delivery before the weekend. (Pause) We're short staffed..."

"I understand that you'd like to pay a lower price. (Pause) Consider the options on this model..."

Suddenly each of these statements sounds more sincere and less like a dismissive excuse.

Slow down and mean it

Deliver the first statement with sincerity and make sure you take a long enough pause between sentences for added impact. Add the appropriate facial gestures. Practise in the mirror a few times and take it for a test drive. Are you buying your reflection?

What a difference!

This is the sign of a Professional Salesperson – someone who is tactful, diplomatic and an expert communicator. Customers won't even know that you omitted the word *BUT*. Though they certainly notice when it's there, they don't miss it when it's gone.

Five steps to cutting out *BUT*

1. Acknowledge your use of the word.

2. Make a commitment to get rid of *BUT*.

3. Practise the statements above in the mirror *without it*.

4. Stop yourself in mid-conversation. Correct yourself when using it (not in front of customers).

5. Agree with a friend to call each other out when you say *BUT.*

The fifth step works extremely well and can actually be fun. Make a bet with a co-worker – whoever uses *BUT* the most from Monday to Thursday has to buy lunch on Friday. The friendly competition will solve the problem in no time. No one wants to lose a bet, and no one likes to be corrected repeatedly for the same mistake.

Once you've masterfully eliminated *BUT* from your vocabulary, your rapport and trust with customers will skyrocket. Suddenly you're communicating genuine empathy and concern for their feelings. Always remember – people are entitled to feel the way they do based on the information they have. The better the information, the better the decision.

Don't stop there!

Don't just use your newfound skill on customers. Removing *BUT* from your dialogue has the same effect in everyday communication with staff, colleagues, friends and family. Sincerity is one of the greatest qualities you can be known for in your relationships with people.

CHAPTER 19
The Prospect of Gain vs. The Fear of Loss

There are many motivators that cause people to take action. There are two very powerful subconscious incentives, though, that are rooted in human behaviour: the prospect of gain and the fear of loss. These two primal motivators form the basis of many decisions.

Let's look at the stock market

We don't have to know much about the stock market to know that for every buyer of a particular stock, there is someone equally motivated to sell it.

The buyer

It's simple. The buyer sees value in the stock at its current price and expects it to increase. That's the *prospect of gain*. Though the determining factors may vary, all buyers of stock share one common agreement: its perceived value. *"This is a good price to pay for this company and I'm motivated to take action to buy it today."* Without buyers, there could be no sellers.

The seller

The seller is motivated by a *fear of loss*. They feel that the current stock price will go down (or have agreed to sell it when it reaches a particular price, a mechanism that is in itself motivated by the fear of loss).

Every day's performance on the stock market is set by the amount and intensity of sellers versus buyers. Both the prospect of gain and fear of loss can be powerful stimulants. Their intensity within us creates a specific sense of urgency to take action. The greater the intensity, the quicker we feel we must act to change our current position of complacency.

Imagine this scenario

Imagine you're a Professional Media Salesperson and you've created a multi-sponsor promotional concept that requires specific businesses to make it work. You reach out to one of the businesses with which you'd like to partner on the initiative and leave a message. In it, you inform the decision-maker that you have an upcoming promotional idea that could offer him great community imaging with his potential target market. In this example, you're playing to his *prospect of gain*.

If you were to add that you want to talk to him first before approaching any of his competitors, you'd now be using the *fear of loss*. This is a real scenario from my days as a Professional Media Salesman. Response was less than overwhelming when I used only the *prospect of gain*. As soon as I introduced the *fear of loss*, I'd receive a call back within 24 hours.

The stronger motivator

Of the two enticements – the prospect of gain and fear of loss – one is far more powerful than the other (for most people).

The fear of loss compels us to take action more often and more quickly than the prospect of gain. The advertising industry plays on this anxiety with limited time offers, incentives and deadlines.

Fear of loss at its finest:

Black Friday and Boxing Day sales

Door-crasher specials

Limited-time incentives

The rare pre-owned vehicle at the car dealership

Radio station contests

Investment deadlines for tax deductions

The job opportunity of a lifetime

Last boarding announcements at airports

Proposing to that special someone

Using these motivators in sales

Professional Salespeople use a combination of both prospect of gain and fear of loss to encourage people to make positive decisions. Once you've identified the key needs of your customer, start with the *prospect of gain*. Show them the advantages of buying your product or service. Understand what is important to them and what they would find most beneficial.

Recognize their buying signs by the questions they ask and the concerns they express. Once this has been established, you may realize that the *fear of loss* will play a strong part in the decision to proceed.

Don't make this mistake!

Don't be the salesperson that attempts to use the fear of loss at the outset. This is a sign of an inexperienced salesperson who is *trying to close you*. Invest the time in developing a relationship of rapport and trust before introducing the fear of loss. Use it sincerely and sparingly with the customer's best interests at heart.

Warning - don't neglect the fear of loss!

Just as you shouldn't drive home the fear of loss right from the start, it's equally important to not neglect it entirely. This is vital.

If your product or service is in short supply, or a deadline is approaching, you'd best make sure that your interested customer is *fully aware* of it. Missing out on an opportunity that the customer *actually wanted* never ends well for anyone – and that includes you as the salesperson! When this happens, the customer will often break their relationship with you and buy elsewhere out of anger. That means you've done all the hard work and get nothing for your efforts.

You must ensure that you educate potential customers with such information. Remember to use the appropriate timing. Don't introduce *fear of loss* until the customer has shown interest through their engagement with you.

CHAPTER 20
Servicing your Customer After the Sale

As you've become aware in this book, I love to relate real life experiences that I've had. It's the basis of my learning. Without these incidents, I wouldn't have the knowledge or practical application to write this book. Here's one of the best learning experiences a client ever taught me:

Meet "Gavin"

Gavin was one of my best clients; a pleasure to work with, straightforward and professional. Though he was demanding, he was easy to please because he made clear exactly what he needed in order to continue purchasing my products and services as an advertising account manager (a fancy name for Professional Media Salesperson).

The start of our relationship

Before I knew Gavin, I prospected him and managed to gain an appointment. After doing a thorough needs analysis, I knew what he needed to justify starting a buying relationship with me. He was open, sincere and had high expectations.

The creative strategy

I did my homework, pooled the resources at my disposal and created an advertising strategy that even I was impressed with – no small task given the high expectations I had of myself. It was important to me that my clients signed contracts based on results, not just because they liked my personality.

The engagement

I had several meetings with Gavin to explain my strategy long before I ever delivered a proposal. I've always maintained that your proposal should never contain anything unexpected. It should just be a confirmation of everything discussed and already agreed to. From the client's perspective, it makes the contract incredibly tough not to sign! I took Gavin for lunch a few times, always paid the bill against his desire, and made sure he felt appreciated and engaged. I even threw him a few perks that came my way. It was hard not to like him.

The marriage

After all the details of my strategy had been confirmed and nothing appeared to be unresolved, I presented a proposal to Gavin for a 13-week advertising campaign. He absolutely loved it. In fact, he said it was the best marketing and advertising strategy he'd ever seen. I could tell he was proud of me, almost like a father recognizing his son for his hard work and diligence. He signed the deal without any negotiating whatsoever.

The honeymoon

Gavin signed on for 13 weeks and the campaign performed far beyond anyone's expectations. Gavin claimed he could tell when a radio commercial aired on my station because his phone lines would light up with potential customers wanting more information. In fact, he asked to know in advance when the commercials would air so he could properly staff his phones!

The happy relationship

At the end of the 13-week strategy, Gavin quickly signed on for a full 52-week term. He was now one of my five biggest accounts, coming out of nowhere literally four months prior. Once again, he signed the contract with no negotiating. Though I was actually shocked, I did my best to hide my surprise. Gavin claimed that the idea I'd brought him was the *best thing that ever happened to his company.* Wow. I'd thought a high paycheque was my biggest inspiration in professional sales. Hearing a client say that, though, provided a form of payment that money couldn't match. *I was making a real difference in this company's revenues!*

The three-month check-up

I would call Gavin every three months. There really wasn't much need to, as he paid his bills with great discipline. *"Hey Gavin!"* I'd say. *"It's Dave calling. How's everything going? Is the campaign still performing well?"* Then I'd hear something like this:

"You bet Dave. Like clockwork. Best thing we ever did. How are you doing by the way?"

Everything with Gavin had been humming along smoothly. I had turned off my proactive efforts to other clients who were in need of my services. I mean really, what was Gavin going to do? *Cancel the best thing his company ever did?*

The renewal

Eventually the 52-week advertising campaign with Gavin was coming up for renewal. I thought I'd take him for lunch like old times. My week was busy with new appointments and other projects on the go, so I thought, *"You know, I'll take him for lunch after the deal is signed."*

I called him. *"Gavin, you might be aware that our strategy is coming for your renewal shortly. I assume everything's still working well for you?"* *"It certainly is Dave, come on by and let's get it signed before I start spending my budget elsewhere!"*

"Man, this is the easiest key account renewal I've had in my career," I thought.

The signing

I presented Gavin with the proposal and he asked me for my pen. As I passed it to him, I said, *"Gavin, I'm just happy that I could be involved in creating this strategy. It gives me such satisfaction to see the results from our work together."* He replied, *"Me too Dave. You know how I feel about it. I've told you many times over."*

The shock of my career

Gavin signed the proposal and didn't ask for a discount. Instead, he gave me one of the biggest lessons of my career. He crossed out "52 weeks" and wrote "13 weeks" in its place. He initialled the change, turned the proposal back to me and asked me to do the same.

My reaction

I was dumbfounded. What was I missing? Why in the world would he do this? The campaign had always exceeded expectations and was one of the reasons for the company's huge growth in sales. I looked up at him. *"Sorry Gavin, am I missing something?"* The look on my face must have been priceless from someone who makes it a policy to always be prepared for curve balls.

Gavin's next words

"Well Dave," he said, *"your campaign strategy has always been successful – from the start to this very day. You worked hard putting it together and deserve every penny of the commission. I'm agreeing to 13 weeks because maybe I might see you a little more often around here. I think you'll call me and take me for lunch, and maybe let me pay the bill. That's all."* Then he smiled and looked at me with that sorry-but-I-felt-I-had-to-do-that face.

My embarrassment

The warm rush of blood red to my face was like nothing I've ever felt. I was horrified at myself for what I had allowed to happen. I had focused on the *results* and not on the *person*. I'd pursued him, done my due diligence, confirmed the business and moved onto the next client, all the while thinking, *"What's he going to do – CANCEL?"*

The Dave that he knew before the sale was not the same Dave he experienced *after the sale*. After far too many apologies, I told him that he'd just taught me a lesson that I would remember – and *share* with others – for decades. I thanked him for teaching me something that I would never forget.

Thank you Gavin!

The take-away

I know you get it. Now *never forget it*. Learn from my mistake: *Never take your clients for granted.* Give them the same service *after the sale* as you did courting them to get the sale. Tell them that you appreciate their business. Show up once in a while *without* a strategy, a request for money or some other agenda.

Bring their staff some coffee and treats occasionally. Only calling your clients when you want to sell them something is dialing for dollars. Partner with your clients. Think like them. Forward them great articles and blog posts that relate to their business category or personal interests. All great relationships can grow stronger.

The best form of value-add you can provide your clients comes from outside your direct buying relationship. *It shows that you care beyond your personal agenda of making a sale.*

CHAPTER 21
The 5 Steps to Leaving Professional Voice Mail Messages

I know you've left a voice mail message that you wish you could take back and do over. This typically happens when you're pressed for time, dial someone's number and then get mentally distracted. You finish the message shaking your head wondering if you should leave another one to try to make up for the first.

Professional Salespeople adhere to the following five steps to leave great voice mail messages every time.

Step #1 – Collect your thoughts

 Before you pick up the phone, take a moment to think your message through. What do you wish to accomplish? Jot down a couple of key words or numbers if required. One moment of preparation can result in a clear, concise voice mail message that makes a great impression. Your message stands a better chance of being returned quickly by simply clearing your head before dialing the number.

Step #2 – Use the person's name – twice

 Everyone loves the sound of their own name, even if they don't know the person saying it. So start your message with the recipient's name. End it with a polite thank you followed by – you guessed it – their name. Professional Salespeople are in the industry of making great impressions. Why not use every tool at your disposal?

Step #3 – Slow down and enunciate

This is one of the biggest mistakes in leaving voice mail messages. Let me give you an example.

*HiMichaelIt'sMarkcallingfromABCComputersYouasked
metocheckosomeinformationtheotherdaywhenyouwalked
inthestoreImanagedtofindoutthatwehavetheprinteryouare
lookingforinourotherstoreCallmeatninesixthreetwenny
fivetwelfthanks.*

We've all received messages like this. You know, the ones you have to play back three times to figure out the number? Once I even had to ask someone else to listen to a message to help me decipher it. In the end, I didn't return the message because neither of us could figure it out.

Slow down and enunciate, pronouncing your words carefully. Try to find a happy medium between the delivery above a-n-d s-o-u-n-d-i-n-g l-i-k-e y-o-u j-u-s-t s-t-a-r-t-e-d y-o-u-r f-i-r-s-t l-e-s-s-o-n i-n r-a-d-i-o a-n-n-o-u-n-c-e-r s-c-h-o-o-l.

Professional Salespeople are natural with their delivery and deliver their message with a cheerful, enthusiastic tone. Regardless of what anyone says, you most definitely can hear a smile!

A valid business reason

If you're leaving a prospecting message, leaving a *valid business reason* with a *sense of urgency* will greatly increase your chance of a call back. A valid business reason is, as it sounds, a reason for your call. If you're trying to book an appointment with a new prospect, leaving a message that says you're going to be in the client's area on a specific day does nothing to motivate her to call you back.

Telling her that your company has found a way to save businesses like hers 25% on her printing costs with quicker turnaround time and green environmental options stands a much better chance of a call back.

Ensure your valid business reason and sense of urgency is sincere, and from the buyer's perspective – *not yours.* There's an easy way to distinguish between the two. If your valid business reason is based around you or your company, it's not client focused.

Understand that no one cares about your schedule, your new product or your latest creation. Customers care about things that matter to them. Get inside their head. That's the basis of a strong valid business reason.

Should you leave a message?

They may not return your call. Then why leave a message anyway? Throughout my sales career, I've always left messages on prospecting calls. It's a first impression and better than none at all. It's the start of what you're hoping to create – a relationship.

Besides, what are your other options? Keep calling at different times of the day in hopes of reaching them without leaving a message? Can you really afford to waste your time playing games of cat and mouse? We'll discuss different ways to reach out to clients who don't return your calls in chapter 27.

Step Four – Repeat your name and contact number

 Professional Salespeople are experts at making it easy to retrieve voice mail. Starting with your name and phone number is proper telephone etiquette as an introduction to your customer. Repeating it at the end is professional courtesy. It means your client doesn't have to replay your message to write down the number.

At the start of your message, pronounce the last four digits of your phone number as separate numbers. So for example, 963-2512 will sound like "nine six three, two five one two." At the end of your message, repeat the last four numbers as a group of two. So 963-2512 becomes nine six three, twenty-five, twelve. This allows the customer's ear to recognize the numbers two different ways for better accuracy.

Step Five – 30 seconds, no more!

 No one wants to hear a two-minute voice mail message. Business owners and decision-makers are potentially reviewing many voice mail messages at once, and it's not something they look forward to. Then there's the decision of which messages to return first. Don't give your customers a reason to roll their eyes and skip over your message because of its length.

Professional Salespeople leave voice mail messages that are *no longer than 30 seconds* from start to finish. If there are a lot of details to communicate, simply tell the customer that you're sending an email with all the necessary information. Take it upon yourself to make it easy to communicate and do business with you.

A voice mail to prioritize your email

I've had tremendous success leaving voice mail messages informing customers that I'm sending them an email with all the information they requested. They actually make my email a priority amongst the many waiting in their Inbox!

A great example of a professional voice mail message

Hi Michael! It's Mark calling from ABC Computers. 963-2512 (nine six three - two five one two). Great news! After some searching, I found the printer that you're looking for. I've reserved it for you for the next 24 hours. Please call me at 963-2512 (nine six three - twenty five twelve). Thanks Michael!

Voice mail yourself

Chances are good that you've never done this. *I highly recommend you do.* Practise leaving professional voice mail messages to yourself. Then play them back to hear things that you've never heard before. Be prepared to not like the sound of your voice! It's natural to be critical of hearing yourself at first. Continue to practise adding the right amount of enthusiasm, pacing and enunciation.

If you think this is silly, ask yourself this question: *"Would a Professional Salesperson who wants to be an expert at creating great impressions do something like this?"*

The answer is *"Yes."*

CHAPTER 22
The Best Use of Email

If you're a Professional Salesperson, email is just one more method at your disposal for reaching out to new potential customers. Used properly, and in the right context, it can be very effective.

Yes, we all know that *face-to-face contact* is vital in establishing strong relationships with customers, co-workers and bosses. There is simply no replacement for it. You also have to be careful not to let email take over your workday – it has a sneaky tendency to expand into any free minute if you let it.

With these caveats in mind, let's look at the different types of email Professional Salespeople send and receive and how to best deal with it.

Prospecting for new business

 When reaching out to new contacts for business development, we've all heard this:

"Why don't you put some information together and send me an email?"

Inexperienced salespeople take this as a positive sign that the customer may have some interest. A request for an email sounds like a sincere request for further discussion, doesn't it? Maybe.

Professional Salespeople also know that if your customer is located in the same general geographic location as you, they will likely not agree to buy your product or service without a *face-to-face appointment*. Though this does depend somewhat on the type of product or service you're selling and its price point, we all tend to require at least one meeting to make a decision to move forward. While it can be done, it's extremely difficult to establish rapport and build trust without a meeting.

Who really wants another email?

Here's the best way I've learned to counter the send-me-an-email objection:

"May I ask you a question?" (Wait for the answer, as this is permission to proceed)

"How many emails do you receive in a day?" (Wait for the answer)

"Do you really want another one? It's my job to simplify things for you, not add to your workload. Frankly, I'm not even sure I can help you or if my services are suited to you. Why don't we get together? We can mutually exchange information and educate each other. The better the information you have, the better the decisions you'll make. Does that sound fair?" (Wait for a potential answer and then ask for the appointment)

"Is there a particular day or time that works best for you?

The results

If delivered professionally and sincerely, this response will convince 90% of your prospects to book an appointment. When I started my sales career, I would eagerly send out emails and then be forced to play the game of cat and mouse. When I was a buyer, I would use the send-me-an-email objection to simply get rid of salespeople. It worked better than any other method I could find.

What if it doesn't work?

There are, however, some customers who will require you send an email first before setting up an appointment. There are many different reasons they might give you, the most common one being, *"I'd like to review the information first, thank you."*

My response

"I understand. I'll send it to you today with the subject line, 'Your request for more information.' That will make it easy to spot in your Inbox. I'll be sending it to you today. When do you think you might be able to review it?" (Wait for the answer)

"What's a good day and time to call you back to answer any questions you have?"

Be sure to call back *on that exact day and at that exact time*. Not five minutes earlier, not five minutes later. You have a phone appointment to arrange a face-to-face appointment.

Your email

Send a brief email with the benefits of what your product or service is and a brief explanation of its features – nothing more. The longer the email, the greater the chance of it not being read.

Busy decision-makers like brief bullet points, so get to the point and don't ramble on. Full paragraphs and lengthy detail give customers a reason to disregard your email and subsequent follow-up call. Impress them with your email and they might actually read it and accept your phone call for a face-to-face appointment.

Your follow-up call

Start your follow-up call to the buyer or gatekeeper by saying that you were asked to call back at this date and time. The gatekeeper will put you through. When you speak to the customer, repeat the same line for him/her.

"Hi (name), it's Dave calling back from PROSALESGUY TRAINING. You asked me to call you back today at (time). Did you get the opportunity to review the information in my email?"

"Yes I did."

"Great. When can we get together so I can answer any questions you may have?" Remember, the point of the call is to secure a face-to-face appointment.

What if the answer is "No, I didn't?"

Ask for a face-to-face appointment!

"I understand. Time is something we all lack. Let me better educate you in person. What day and time works for you?"

The purpose

When it comes to prospecting, the purpose of email is to set up a face-to-face conversation. The purpose of a phone call is no different.

Contact with existing clients

 If your client prefers to communicate via email, make it brief and ensure your subject line captures the crux of the message. Tell them what's required at the start of the email and use the title *"Action Required"* when truly warranted.

Again, I strongly suggest that actual conversations are far more effective than email. Let an email confirm the discussion you just had with the client for record-keeping and detail orientation when needed. In most situations, a phone call can take far less time than thinking of how to word an email to ensure proper communication.

Internal communication

If you don't like to receive dozens of emails a day from within your building, then don't send them. *Get up off your chair, walk over to someone and have a discussion.* Only use the "cc" function when really required. Don't get click-happy and cover your behind.

As an added bonus, walking through your building makes you visible and gets you in front of people. People can feel the warmth of a simple smile down the hallway. You'll also burn a few calories. What's so wrong with that?

Use email sparingly

Here's the general rule: if you can eliminate an email with a face-to-face discussion or phone call, always do so. There will never be a replacement for face-to-face contact – externally or internally. Professional Salespeople know this to their core. You can't build a relationship through email.

CHAPTER 23
Having the Tough Conversations with Clients

Having tough conversations with clients is something that every Professional Salesperson eventually learns to do. Without the courage to have those tough conversations, you will constantly be in reactionary mode. Your clients will call the shots and play the authoritative role in your relationship with them. Be aware that though they take charge, *you* will be held responsible for the results of the relationship.

A learned skill

Having the ability to initiate tough conversations with clients is not something that comes naturally to inexperienced salespeople. In fact, it's a challenge for even the most experienced Professional Salespeople. On one hand, you want to be able to communicate freely with your clients and look out for their best interests. On the other, you understand that they have the power to fire you from their buying relationship. These discussions require sincerity and tact.

Subjects for discussion

Tough conversations can cover any number of topics. Here are a few of the most common:

Payment terms, specifically cash on demand vs. net 30.
Collecting receivables on overdue accounts.
Correcting client perceptions and stigmas that are incorrect.
Informing the client that they are buying the wrong product based on their needs.
Informing the client that they are buying a product for the wrong reasons.
Giving the client full disclosure even when they didn't ask for it.
Dealing with clients who treat your staff improperly.
Dealing with clients who are not telling the truth.
Dealing with clients who have unrealistic expectations.

Every Professional Salesperson has dealt with these and many more difficult issues.

Look at it this way

For years, I would do my best to steer clear of these conversations however possible. My first thought was always, *"It's tough enough to entice a new client, so why would I want to bring up one of these topics and risk losing this one?"*

You have no choice

In many situations, you have no choice. It's part of doing business. If your accounting department says your newly landed client is cash on demand, it's your job to explain the situation. And believe it or not, that's a good thing!

What's so good about it?

Every time you have to initiate one of these uncomfortable conversations you become better at it. Like it or not, it's something you will have to do repeatedly in your sales career. The sooner you learn how to do it properly, the better.

The approach

Make the discretionary call knowing your client's personality and character. The direct approach works far better than most, yet your wording and diplomacy is key. You want to be forthright and honest. You also want to be sensitive to the client's reaction and emotional state so that you can motivate them to embrace your solution.

The challenge

You're delivering two very different and distinct messages. First, here are the facts and realities. Second, here's the solution and remedy to the situation. Dealing with the facts quickly allows you to move on to the remedies sooner.

Your client will not be pleased with the first part of your communication. Expect that and give them time to vent. Just actively listen and don't offer any defences. Allow them to be emotional – if you rob them of that, they will make sure to dwell on it when you're ready to talk solutions. "Let the wind blow through town" is one of my favorite expressions .

Once your client has had the opportunity to vent, you have a chance to engage them in finding a workable remedy to the situation. Professional Salespeople use every skill at their disposal to motivate their client to focus on the solution, not the problem. Your positive attitude and relationship skills will come in very handy.

Years ago, a mentor taught me a very apt analogy for this process. Anyone who knows me has likely heard this comparison many times.

The Brick in the Pillow

The issue you have to discuss with your client is the brick. You could take the brick and smack your client in the head with it and get the job done. *Let's just get this over with fast!* Whack, there you go. While that will certainly get your point across, however, consider the potential damage.

Could you cause their skin to be broken, blood to spill, break bones and maybe cause a concussion?

Do you really think your relationship will endure that trauma?

The solution, as you've probably guessed, is to put the brick in a pillow with some soft feathers around it. Now wind up and deliver the message. No blood, no bruising, no concussion – maybe just a slight headache afterward. The message was still communicated directly, yet the feathers of the solution softened its impact. I've used this technique for decades and it works amazingly.

 Professional Salespeople become very talented at navigating tense situations once they figure out the "Brick and Pillow formula."

The Brick and Pillow formula:

 The Size of The Brick = The Severity of the Issue that Needs to be Communicated.
The Amount of Feathers = How Hard you Wish the Client to Perceive the Impact.

Your goal is to ensure the client gets the message and has an eventual desire to focus on the solution. Here are a few factors you need to consider:

The personality and volatility of the client.
Is the Brick a stand-alone issue or part of a much bigger Brick Wall that needs to be discussed?
Have you already had this discussion with the client before?
What are your personal feelings toward this client?

Here's a tough example: cash on demand

You: *(Client name), it appears our accounting department is asking for payment up-front.*

Client: *Excuse me?*

You: *The accounting department would like you to pay COD.*

Client: *Really. Well isn't that special. You would be the only supplier I have that requires that. Why? What was in the credit application? Frankly, I'm not impressed. Are you saying I'm a bad credit risk?*

You: *Not at all. Our company has the most stringent procedures of our industry. I understand. I would have the same reaction if I heard what you just did. I have no idea why they said this. They seldom go into details. They would just prefer if you paid COD.*

Client: *Well, why would I do that when every one of your competitors gives me net 30, if not net 60 or even up to 90 days to pay the bill? What makes you so special that I should pay you up front? Who do I have to talk to to change this?*

You: *The best person to talk to is me in all of your matters. I'm your salesperson and am responsible for your account. I understand you're upset. At some point, I'd like to tell you my solution and how we can deal with this and move forward.*

Client: *(Pause) And how might that be?*

You: *We accept three different forms of credit card. If you simply pay for the product as you request it monthly, you will be paying as you proceed. A lot of my clients pay this way. They still earn points on their purchases and, frankly, many of them prefer paying this way. One of my clients actually goes to Hawaii each year based on this payment method.*

Client: *What If I don't have a corporate credit card?*

You: *You can certainly use a personal card and take as long as you want to pay the balance. It's up to you. If that doesn't work, some of my clients write post-dated cheques each month. Again, you pay as you go. Many clients like this method because the money is out of their account without their payables stacking up month after month eating away at their profits. It's up to you which method you think works best for you.*

The accounting department *loved me* at every company I worked at. They even admitted to breaking credit procedures for me because of my ability to collect. I never had a client who broke their relationship with me because of COD payment. I would even tell my clients this:

"Look, if you pay this way, you will never get a call from me asking for money. I'd rather focus my creativity and hard work on ideas that grow your business. My job is to be part of your business solutions, not be a bill collector."

Brick in a Pillow. Works like a charm. Have the confidence to have the tough conversations with your clients and they'll appreciate you more for it. You'll also earn an enormous amount of self-respect, which is better than cash in the bank. Well, almost.

CHAPTER 24
Collaborating with the Buying Committee

In many cases, the person who appears to be in charge of making the buying decisions isn't the only person involved. This person may, in fact, simply be a "gatekeeper" or "screener." In other cases, it may be someone to whom the manager or purchasing agent has delegated the responsibility of supplier research. Though it's very possible that the person in front of you may have little influence on the final decision, *never* do they have *no* influence.

Your ability to recognize who makes the final buying decisions will save you a ton of time and help focus your efforts in the right direction. Professional Salespeople know how to get in front of, and collaborate with, the buying committee – and that knowledge greatly increases their chance of success.

Be careful!

Professional Salespeople know the power of the gatekeeper – they have every opportunity to shut you down cold and put you in a position of weakness. Rub them the wrong way and you will be automatically disadvantaged. *Isn't your job difficult enough?*

Three goals when communicating with a gatekeeper:

1. Respect the role of the gatekeeper and your relationship with him/her.

2. Do nothing to create conflict with this key person.

3. Find out who is on the buying committee and is responsible for the final decision.

OK, so how do I accomplish that?

The short answer is *"with tact and diplomacy."* Understand that the gatekeeper – your contact – has the ability to influence the buying committee. The slightest comment from your contact person can sway opinion either way with the true decision maker(s). Either of the following comments, for example can have a huge impact one way or the other:

"This salesperson was impolite, late with the information and had a real ego."

"This salesperson was extremely professional. She asked great questions and is eager for the business."

What can happen if you aren't careful?

It's important to find out who is responsible for making the buying decision. If you approach this improperly, though, here's what your contact person will perceive:

 "Oh, I get it. You want to know who really makes the decisions around here so you can quickly go around me. Nice. I already don't like you and your agenda."

Over the years, I've developed a system for reaching all three goals within tight timelines. This system works for *all sales situations* – whether you're a Professional Salesperson dealing with a large, publicly traded company or meeting a prospect at a local coffee shop.

Don't assume!

Ask a woman shopping for a car by herself what her experience has been. There are Professional Salespeople who are skilled in dealing with the power of the purchasing female. Then there are those who really could use some training in this area.

 A rookie media salesman I once knew walked into a business on a casual prospecting call. When greeted by a pleasant young woman who asked how she could help, the salesman inexplicably blurted out that he was "looking for the boss, not the office girl." You can probably see where this is going. Of course, the young woman *was* the boss. She quickly sent the offending salesman packing and placed an angry call to the salesman's manager. That one gaffe not only cost the salesman that account; it also cost him his job.

I can't believe this still needs to be said in this day and age: never underestimate the female influence in *all* buying decisions – even for products and services used exclusively by *men*.

The buying committee

Often your contact person will also be a decision-maker. Here's my three-step system for dealing with the buying committee:

Step One - Deal with the person who says they make the decisions

During your first appointment or contact, treat them as if they are the final decision-maker. If you respect their role, they may reveal to you exactly what their responsibility is. They may even tell you the protocol the company follows when making its final choices. Be respectful, establish rapport and earn trust.

Step Two - At the end of the appointment, ask this question:

"(Name), is there anyone in addition to you who might influence the final decision? Or is this 100% your responsibility?"

Step Three - If they share some information about the buying committee, suggest this:

"(Name), I realize this is an important decision for you to make and why it's one of your priorities. It's my job to give you the best information to make the best decisions. Knowing that there are a few people involved, would it be OK if we all got together to discuss possible strategies? Is that fair?"

You don't ever want to make the person you're dealing with feel that you're trying to go around them. Instead, be sure to involve them in all key decisions – their ego is far less likely to get bruised. You have to be very careful with your wording of the above. You must be sensitive and show respect for their role within the company.

What if I get the cold shoulder?

They may not give you a name or inform you of other people involved. They may insist that you deal with them only. If so, *continue onward.* You might say this:

"(Name), I understand. I just want to do my best to help you. I understand you're my contact and the person I should be dealing with."

This shows respect and submits to the directions of your contact. Remember, you must play nice if you want to be allowed to proceed. *Don't be a jerk!*

Don't stop asking

At some point in the future, your contact may suggest that he has to talk with the other people involved in the decision. This presents another opportunity to try to meet the buying committee and key decision-makers. You could say:

"(Name), do you think it might be OK if I join you in having that discussion with the others? That way, if they have any questions I can answer them directly. Is that OK with you? I just want to do my best for you."

Persistence pays off

Eventually, you will get the inside track on who the key people are that make final buying decisions. You may even get a chance to meet them. Either way, once your initial contact trusts you and feels that you're worthy of the information, you've found an ally in your efforts.

Sales success centres on many components. Without rapport, trust, timing and the right approach, your product or service may never get serious consideration.

CHAPTER 25
How to Upsell your Current Customers

There are only two ways to improve your billings and revenues: increasing sales from your existing clients (*upselling*) and acquiring new customers *(new business development)*.

Increasing sales volume from existing clients

It's far easier to leverage strong existing relationships to increase your current clients' spend than it is to develop business from new customers. Please don't take that to mean you can neglect new business development!

Professional Salespeople need to be great at both of these tasks to replace lost billings and build revenue growth from year to year.

The Customer's changing needs

If you're selling products and services to consumers (Business to Consumer, or B2C), when is the last time you made a friendly call to your existing customers? Professional Salespeople understand the importance of building relationships with their customers, both to enrich the relationship and encourage more sales.

Professional Salespeople diligently maintain their relationships long after the initial sale is made. Is purchasing your product a once in a lifetime occurrence? Cars, homes, appliances, furniture, cell phones and most products and services are *repeat purchases made several times in a person's lifetime.*

So why aren't you calling your past customers?

Are you scared to call because of buyer's remorse or problems with the product or service? The purchase your customer made shouldn't be treated as a one-time transaction. It has the potential to be so much more.

For Professional B2C Salespeople, continuing a great relationship goes beyond a one-time phone call or a calendar in the mail each year.

Try this

Make the occasional phone call to everyone who purchased from you and say this:

"I just called to see how you're doing. How was your long weekend? Can I mail you a gift card to (coffee shop) to say thanks and show that I appreciate your business? How's your (product or service) working out? I really just called to say hi."

Avoid falling into this quicksand

Don't make every call a *"dialing for dollars call."* Be careful of turning into what your customers perceive most salespeople to be. It can happen quickly with comments like these:

"And by the way, I just wanted to let you know about our big sale this weekend."
"Please keep me in mind if you're every looking to buy again."
"Do you know of anyone looking to buy my product or service?"

I get it

Yes, there will be times when it's smart to call past customers for the obvious reasons of doing your job and soliciting sales. When that time comes, tell your customers that you're *doing your job as a good salesperson and making a shameless self-promotion call.* Be up front about it. Your customer will be fine with it – heck, we all have to make a living. If you're honest and upfront with them, they just might return the gesture.

Don't let *"making the sale"* be the basis of your relationship. Don't be a legal pick-pocket. No one likes that salesperson.

Professional B2B Salespeople

If you're selling products and services to businesses (Business to Business, or B2B), when was the last time you did a full customer needs analysis? Your clients' needs can change unpredictably based on market conditions, timing and many other variables. Your strategy needs to keep pace – you can and should ask a few great questions when you check in with a routine service call.

A long-term renewal always needs a new customer needs analysis. Don't treat your long-term buyers like passing *"Go"* in Monopoly to collect a renewal agreement. Don't forget the lessons of chapter 20 – Servicing your Customers After the Sale!

Remember what I wrote in Chapter 1:

"Professional Salespeople increase their odds of an upsell or repeat purchase when they invest in maintaining an authentic, sincere relationship with their buyers. Just play nice and you will see the return."

CHAPTER 26
Prospecting for New Clients - What Works Best?

Be honest – did you skip ahead to this chapter or did you genuinely read every page up until now?

This is the chapter that entices every salesperson because it addresses the one activity we all know will make or break our business, yet it's also the activity with which most salespeople struggle the most.

Whether B2C or B2B, every Professional Salesperson knows they need to reach out and attract new clients. It's the only way to keep pace with attrition and build revenues year after year.

The siren call of sales technology

With the easy access and widespread use of online information, you will see a great amount of articles and posts making claims like:

Cold Calling is Dead!
Social Media - The Smart Way to Prospect!
How to Reach your Next Customer on LinkedIn!
Inbound Marketing – the New Future of Sales Prospecting!

Many of these statements promise a simple, one-size-fits-all form of reaching out to new customers. It's easy to be influenced by new trends because we all want to stay up-to-date. No one wants to appear out of touch with the "new way" of doing business.

While new initiatives are always worth exploration, it's your job to determine which have the potential to become tried-and-true techniques that warrant inclusion in your arsenal.

My experience

Throughout my career, I've used virtually every method of prospecting. Selling life insurance door-to-door required ringing doorbells and avoiding dogs. In real estate I printed personal sales material and knocked on doors. With Amway, I enticed friends and family with books, sample products and success stories from leaders in the industry.

Media sales demanded cold calling and emailing thousands of business owners in an effort to gain an appointment. Let's not forget to add networking events and business mixers to the list!

In my current sales training and consulting company, I make many friendly calls to past and current clients every week in order to maintain relationships. I'm extremely active on LinkedIn and Twitter, and I blog every week to reach out to new decision-makers. My will and assertiveness have enabled me to do a lot of things that other people might shy away from.

Yes, I've tried virtually every form of prospecting under the sun, and I've learned valuable lessons from every one of them.

So Dave, what works best?

It entirely depends on these factors:

- The nature of your product and its market – B2B or B2C.

- Your knowledge, confidence and skill level in each method of prospecting.

- Your ability to be open-minded, learn new techniques and commit to mastering them.

- Your ability to internalize new concepts and make them yours.

- Your ability to *"suck it up"* and step out of your comfort zone.

The next few chapters are devoted to sharing my experiences with both traditional and new methods of prospecting. I'll share my tips for cold calling, asking for referrals, cultivating your existing personal and professional relationships and harnessing the power of social media – including Facebook, LinkedIn, Twitter, YouTube, Google+ and blogging.

This brings two worlds together. The following information is great if you've just started in Professional Sales or perhaps a veteran of the sales industry.

CHAPTER 27
Cold Calling

Cold calling is one of my favourite ways to find new customers; it can also be one of the toughest.

Why do I enjoy cold calling so much? Probably because I got really good at it over many years as an *"outside"* salesperson. *Outside* salespeople have to actively pursue new customers; *inside* salespeople generally have customers come to them. The better you are at something the more fun it is, right? So why not learn how to be great at cold-calling instead of good at avoiding it?

I've always found cold calling to be one of the most effective ways for B2B salespeople to prospect. Does that surprise you? Yes, it's a numbers game – all prospecting is. As you work your way through all those *No's*, you may get the feeling that no business owners or decision-makers want to talk to you.

Guess what?

They don't. Yet, they are always open to new ideas to increase their profit and market share. They just don't appreciate the huge amount of unsolicited phone calls they get from salespeople, most of which profess to have the best, the fastest, the cheapest or some combination of all three.

Professional Salespeople don't make promises they can't keep. They don't spew out offers and claims to a decision-maker that has shown no interest to date. Why would you do that? How can you commit to anything when you don't even know anything about the business you're calling?

The silly things we say when cold calling...

- *"I have a new idea, concept, strategy or product that will make/ save you money."*

- *"I'm in your area on Tuesday and have some available appointment time."*

- *"I was wondering if you might be interested in my product or service."*

- *"I'm really excited to get together with you."*

What the buyer thinks:

- *"Who cares?"*

- *"Good for you. Book a tee-time at our local golf course."*

- *"No, I'm not interested. If I were, I would have called you."*

- *"You won't be excited for long because it's not going to happen."*

What are you trying to get?

Your goal on a cold call is to book an appointment – *not convince the buyer to purchase!* After all, how do you know yet whether your product or service can even help this company?

Something to think about

On every cold call, a sale is made.

Either you *"sell"* the idea that it's worth the decision-maker's time to book an appointment with you, or the decision-maker *"sells you"* on the idea that it's not. You can take that to the bank. It was one of the greatest things I ever learned about cold calling – someone always wins the call.

Use a script as a guideline

Professional Salespeople don't wing it; they use scripts. I don't mean they *read* them necessarily. They *feel* them. *Internalize* them. They make the script theirs and use it as a framework for a conversational dialogue that doesn't sound like their auditioning for the school play.

The lead-in

Here's a simple lead-in script I often used as a Professional Salesperson that turned many cold calls into appointments. You'll have to adjust the words a bit and customize it for your own personality and product, of course. Once you do, though, it's yours.

Hi (name). It's (your name) calling from (your company).

Pause a second here for recognition. Give them a chance to break the ice. Please don't ask them how they're doing – there's no surer way to set off their salesperson alarm. *Salesperson Alert!*

Did I reach you at a good time?

I know what you're thinking – why would you give them the chance to escape? Look, you want them to at least pay some attention to you. If their mind is occupied, you won't get an appointment anyway. If they say, *"No, it's not a good time,"* ask them when you should call back. That will result in one of two things:

1. An offer of a better time. *"Great, I'll call you back then. Thanks."* No, don't wish them a great day. *Salesperson Alert!* Call them back at the exact time specified. That's you living up to your commitments. *"Hi (name), you asked me to call you back (day) and (time) . . ."*

2. The *"What's this about?"* response. Wonderful. It's game time.

The next step

(Name), you don't know me. We've never met. I came across your business (provide details). Do you mind if I ask you a few quick questions?

I've never received a *"Please do!"* response, and I've also never received a *"Beat it deadbeat."* It usually sounds more like mild indigestion followed by a less than enthusiastic, *"Sure, yeah, OK."*

Are you open to new ideas to (insert a basic vital need here - increasing market share/saving costs on/finding the right staff, etc.?)?

What's the buyer going to say, *No?* It's only happened once in my career. (I thanked the decision-maker for their time and hung up.) You're much more likely to get a lukewarm grunt in response.

(Name), I have no idea if I can help you. I'm not even sure if (my product or service) is good for your business. All I can offer is an appointment to mutually exchange information. You tell me about your business, and I'll tell you about our (product or service). The better the information you have, the better the decisions you make. Does that sound fair?

Why this works

Look at what this opening sequence has accomplished:

- You committed to nothing that might be a challenge to deliver.

- You didn't make silly claims, beating your chest like a sales ape.

- You didn't sound like 99% of the salespeople who called them that week.

- You were sincere, honest and genuine. Rapport-building starts with the cold call!

What happens if they say something like this?

- *"Email me some information."*

- *"I'm in a commitment with another supplier."*

- *"Our budget's spent."*

- *"I'm just on the way to a meeting."*

- *"I'm not interested."*

My response

- *"How many emails do you get in a day? Do you really want another one? I'd like to simplify your job, not make it harder."*

- *"I'm not even sure I can help you. The purpose of getting together is to mutually exchange information, not agree to do business together."*

- *"I understand. If you came across what you truly thought was a great idea, could you find the budget somewhere?"*

- *"I understand. When would be a good time for me to call you back?"*

- *"That makes sense. If you were interested, you would have called me. The reason for the appointment is to mutually exchange information. Nothing more"*

Remember the rules of the script:

Internalize the script. Make it yours. Don't give up.

Someone always wins the cold call. *Who's it going to be?*

De-pressurizer

If you ever feel that you may be getting a little too intense or are pressuring a prospect into a decision, this de-pressurizer works like a charm:

"I'm sorry if I come on a little strong sometimes. I just feel passionate about what I do."

Say it with a smile and, if it fits your personality, maybe even a light-hearted chuckle. This line has always resulted in a smile, often accompanied by a comment like, *"I wish we had more people around here like that,"* or *"Why don't you come sell for us and say that to our clients?"*

Cold call in person or by phone?

I've always done my cold calling on the phone. Use a landline or make sure you have a rock-solid cellular connection – don't trust your first impression with a new client to a shaky mobile network. The advantages of cold calling by phone are clear. You can cover much more ground on the phone than you can visiting in person.

Some Professional Salespeople feel that it's easier to reject you on the phone and much tougher in person. Perhaps so. You can call many more people in an hour than you can visit, however, and so great cold calling skills on the phone will still see you book more appointments.

Stopping by a client's office can also annoy busy decision-makers who hate salespeople who drop by unannounced. *"So what, I'm supposed to drop everything for you just because you walked in?"*

When stopping by makes sense

Here's my cold calling protocol:

1. Make a call.

2. Leave a message (Back it up with an email if you can.)

3. Repeat steps 1 and 2 three times with a few days between each attempt.

4. If the buyer still hasn't responded, *then* stop by. What have you got to lose? Your pride?

5. If nothing works, send them an email like this.

   "I can appreciate how busy you are. It appears the timing of my contact is not the best. I will attempt to re-connect with you in 30 days. Please let me know if this is appropriate."

Come to life

I have actually had prospects *"come to life"* with that email. They usually apologize and initiate a conversation. The second that happens, I ask to book an appointment to explain.

If not, I follow them up in 30 days like clockwork. I have had clients finally call me, giving me praise for my follow up skills.

Persistence virtually always pays off

All decision-makers appreciate creativity, even though they won't admit it. Be careful though – *stalking* a buyer is not a great way to build a relationship.

Mix it up

While you may not be doing anything wrong, you might not be doing something right in your efforts to succeed.

Don't be afraid to try a new approach. Call three times and leave messages. Send three emails. Visit the client. Tell the gatekeeper that you wanted to stop by to set up an appointment with the buyer. If you're told that she schedules her own appointments, ask to see her for one minute to do that.

Send her a card in the mail with a $5 coffee gift card. Be creative. Be resilient. Don't give up too easily. Try back again after a month. Timing can be crucial.

And, of course, the most important point:

Don't take rejection personally!

CHAPTER 28
Engagement - The Key to Making the Sale

Let's say your prospecting efforts have been successful and you have an appointment with a potential client. You're now entering the crucial phase of *engagement*. The engagement phase is equally important for all salespeople, whether you sell professional services to businesses or consumer goods to the public. It's important whether you visit your prospects in their home or business or they come to you. Whatever you're selling, you need to *engage* your customers in a way that makes them *want to* do business with you.

This is where sales are made or lost.

The engagement process can be made up of many steps or just a few. It can last 15 minutes with transactional purchases or 15 months with more complex buying decisions.

After the initial customer needs analysis, it can include further meetings with key individuals within your prospect's company. Consulting with the product development team or the staff members who would actually be using your product or service is sometimes necessary. Rushing the progress and trying to confirm the business with a corny closing technique shows insincerity and can have you out on the street *very fast.*

Shut Up! Please stop talking.

 If you're smart, you aren't yapping about how great your product or service is. I chose the title of this book for a reason. From the start of engagement, the typical stigmatized salesperson *spews* a flurry of product information that turns prospects off and makes them want to run away.

"Who cares? What makes you think that this information is what I'm interested in hearing anyway?"

That's what your customer is thinking if you babble on about anything that they haven't *expressed* interest in hearing. **So zip it**. Professional Salespeople make *The Five Success Skills in chapter five* a part of their natural communication style.

The customer needs analysis

How do you know if your product or service is right for your prospect? With a customer needs analysis – a detailed, specific set of questions that you must ask your prospect. Though the best way to do this is face-to-face, geographical boundaries may necessitate the use of higher technologies, such as phone or, much better, web conferencing.

Dig deep

Don't just ask surface-level questions. Dig deeper to truly find your prospect's specific needs and show your sincerity to help them make the right decision. Deliver a strong opening statement like this:

"I'd like to ask you some questions to make sure I do my best to understand your needs. It's what I do to help my customers make the right decisions. Is that all right with you?"

Once they understand your intent, most clients will be happy to oblige. Your style might be a welcome relief from the chatty salespeople they normally meet with.

Where most sales fail

If the client does not fully partner with you during the engagement phase, your chance of confirming the business is extremely low. *This is exactly where most sales fail*. Professional Salespeople dig deep and probe to find the *real needs* of each client. Refer back to chapter six, in which we discussed the first of Five Success Skills for Professional Salespeople: asking great questions. The right questions will draw out your prospect's true needs. You can then tie those needs to benefits of your product or service and confirm the business.

Remember . . .

The engagement phase isn't just about you engaging your prospect. It's also about getting your prospect to engage with you! Once you feel that your prospect is engaged, you can *sense* the sale taking shape and coming close to approval.

It will be music to your ears. Your customer will ask you questions like:

"When can I start?"

"When would the product arrive?"

"What forms of payment do you accept?"

"What's the next step in the process?

Sales Superstars are so skilled at engaging their customers, and drawing them into engaging with them, that they seldom ever have to use a closing technique. *Clients close themselves.* Now *that* is the sign of a true Professional Salesperson!

Once the sale is made

Don't think for a second that your job is complete when you receive the approval to purchase. Your sale now continues its evolution. Here are some questions you need to ask yourself:

"How do I ensure that everyone on my product team delivers on the commitments I made?"

"How do I continue to give my client the same great service that I provided while enticing them?"

"How do I turn this customer into one of my best ones?"

"How do I ensure that I will get a renewal on our agreement?"

"How will I turn them into one of my leading advocates?"

"How and when will I ask them for referrals?"

Get it? Your job has just started. Hey, now you're earning a commission – and that sure beats working for free!

CHAPTER 29
Asking for Referrals

Please give this chapter the respect it deserves. When I sold life insurance, it was drilled into me to ask for referrals. It was the lifeblood of the industry and the primary source of new business. Though this is true in many categories besides life insurance, only a handful of salespeople ask for referrals.

Even fewer do it properly.

How not to ask for referrals

You: *(Name of great client), do you know of anyone who might be interested in my services?"*

Client: *I'm not sure off hand. Why don't you give me some of your cards and I'll hand them out to anyone who might have an interest.*

You: *Thanks (name)! Here are 10.*

Client: *Why don't you just give me five? I'll let you know if I need more.*

Wait!

Don't order a new car based on how many cards you've handed out. While your client might have a genuine interest in referring business to you, by tomorrow they will have forgotten about their intentions. If someone calls them and asks for a recommendation, they'll probably remember the conversation. Chances are, though, that your card won't be within reach. If you're lucky, they're in your client's desk drawer. Most likely, they've already been tossed.

When Professional Salespeople ask for referrals, they always go one step further.

How Professional Salespeople ask for referrals

You:

(Name of great client), have I ever made you aware that I work on commission? While that strikes fear in most people's hearts, I know you understand what that means. I'm paid on performance. If I don't do my job and keep my customers happy, I don't make a living.

To be successful, I have to reach out to new potential customers. The best way to do that is to ask for referrals from my best clients; the ones who know me, trust me and know I'm not going to harass and stalk their business contacts. I'm looking for people who would actually benefit from meeting me and who might want to develop a relationship like ours.

Do you know of anyone like that? (Discuss with your client whom they have in mind and why they think they would be a great fit.)

Now, there are two ways we could do this. I could call them and say that you referred me to them. Yet there's another way that I think would be more comfortable for everyone. Do you think you'd be willing to take a minute to call them and ask if they'd like to meet me?

Does that make sense? I know your time is valuable - any effort you make is appreciated.

Note, if there are elements of this script that aren't you, then modify them, internalize them and make them yours. Just don't detract from the goal of encouraging clients to make the referral call *for you*.

One referral like this is GOLD

You might be surprised how many of your trusted clients will help you out in this way. Nothing is more powerful than a referral from a trusted source to a colleague!

Imagine the effect the following call will have on a new prospect:

Your client: *Look, I've known (your name) for a long time. She's great. Works hard. Always delivers. She's one of those salespeople that's actually worth meeting with. Do you think you could use her services?*

Now ask yourself this: when you call that person to try to schedule an appointment, is it truly going to be a *cold* call or a *warm* call?

This type of referral is worth 10 typical referrals. At least.

Professional Salespeople are assertive and believe in what they offer their customers. Asking for referrals is a sign of confidence in your product, your service and what you have to offer. Never be ashamed to ask for referrals.

When Professional Salespeople ask for referrals

Wait for the right timing. Do it on the heels of success - *when your client pays you a great compliment.* This is a perfect opportunity to ask for referrals. Your client's mind is open for suggestion. They've just given you credit for a job well done. It's time to leverage your hard work to a another customer. Please don't miss this chance by not having the confidence to ask.

You will miss 100% of the shots you don't take

That comment is courtesy of the great Wayne Gretzky. He also said that his key to scoring goals was that he skated to where he thought the puck was *going to be* – not where it is. He may have been talking hockey, yet his attitude is characteristic of all leaders in any field.

CHAPTER 30
Your Personal and Business Relationships

Professional Salespeople are always on the job. Here's what I mean:

Even when you're not at work, you need to be always interested in meeting new people. Once new contacts have met you and learned they can trust you, they will be receptive to opportunities to do business together.

You are a customer

Think of all the different products and services you buy from Professional Salespeople. Now consider this: every one of these salespeople is a potential customer for you.

Careful!

Let's be clear. I didn't say that you should try to sell your product or service to everyone you know. I think we've all met someone like that. You know, the guy who attends a business function and passes out 100 cards? Or the *"friend"* who manages to steer every conversation toward the great product she's selling? Gee, I wonder where they end up?

What I'm suggesting is that you turn your Professional Salesperson's radar on and ask yourself, *"Would this person be a good potential customer for me in the future?"*

If so, wait for the appropriate moment to bring it up. Sales success is largely about timing.

A message for the leery

Sales is not for shy, timid people. Do you think telling your friends, family and social acquaintances that you're interested in their business *when they're ready* is too assertive?

If so, you might be in the wrong business.

How would these scenarios make you feel?

- The neighbour you occasionally wave to drives home in a new car bought from a salesperson he met at the same car dealership you sell for.

- Your drycleaner for the past 10 years is so excited about her dream vacation to Europe. She met a travel agent at a function last week and booked it the next day. She didn't know that you're a travel consultant at another agency.

- The sales manager makes a special announcement at the sales meeting. One of your colleagues has made a huge sale to a client who controls the business budget for five retail outlets. He called your company asking for a salesperson. The General Manager is the same guy you chat with at your kid's hockey practice every Saturday morning.

It happens every day

These missed opportunities happen to every salesperson in the industry. Yes, they've even happened to me. We miss out on what could have been an *"easy"* sale simply because we were afraid of being too assertive.

Then I've seen salespeople call up their clients after an "oops" like that and make it even worse. It goes something like this . . .

"I heard you bought (product or service). Yeah, I guess I should've told you that I sell those too."

Nice – NOT!

What's that? The Guilt Close for a future sale?

Here's a better way:

"I heard you bought (product or service). You're going to love it. It's a great product. You know, I'm an idiot. (laugh) I never told you that I actually sell them. It's not your fault. (laugh) It's 100% mine. I should've told you. If you ever know of someone else who might be interested, I'd be happy to help."

Move on

Here's another great lesson in sales:

Hindsight is always 20/20. If you look at your mistakes and learn from them, you develop a keener sense of *foresight.*

That's one of my strongest life principles.

Sales self-promotion without the agony

So how do you make the people around you aware that you sell a particular product or service without feeling overly cheesy? The following script, or something very close to it, has always worked well for me:

"I'm always interested in doing business with you, if and when you're ready. Just let me know. I'd be happy to help you."

There. How hard was that?

.

CHAPTER 31
The Five Steps to Turn your Worst Customer into your Best Salesperson

Professional Salespeople take pride in the great customer service they provide. However, even the best of us make the occasional "*oops*" – an unfortunate situation that you'd like to take back and do over. The bad customer experience may not have involved you directly. It may have been the result of someone else within your organization that didn't meet expectations. Regardless, *you* are your client's point person, and it's *you* who will be held accountable. That's the reality of the occupation.

How are you looking at it?

The key to turning a negative experience into a positive one is to recognize the opportunity *to erase a bad customer experience with great service by solving the problem.* The following is my five-step procedure for turning displeased customers into your biggest fans.

Step #1 – Shut up, listen and wait

 You're dealing with a disappointed customer, and that customer is probably upset. The last thing they want to hear right now is the sound of your voice. They need to voice their frustration; your job is to *actively listen.* Don't interrupt. Don't offer explanations. Your client doesn't want to hear them right now.

Sound familiar? This is the same approach you take when you have to initiate an uncomfortable conversation. Believe me, approaching an angry client after a mistake has been made can be a *very* uncomfortable conversation!

Allow them to get it all out

Your client needs the opportunity to vent. Give them reassurance that you are actively listening. In person, that consists of a look of patient concern for their situation with the occasional nod of your head. On the phone, do the same with verbal recognition. The two words *"I understand"* have amazing power in this process. If your client is venting in public, try to move the conversation to an area where you can allow them to let go of their emotions without other customers around.

What, no fight?

Eventually, the disgruntled customer will stop. They'll realize that you're not offering any challenge or willingness to dispute them. *Suddenly they realize that you care.* They will stop arguing, become calm and appear willing to listen. They've now disassociated you with the problem(s) they experienced, even if you were the one who dropped the ball. That's amazing in itself, isn't it?

You now have the privilege of addressing their concerns. They may even ask for your opinion, clearly giving you a signal that it's time for you to talk.

Step #2 – Paraphrase what you heard and felt

 The masters of conflict resolution are experts at paraphrasing. When done properly, it has a huge impact. You are now repeating back to the customer why they are upset and how they feel. No angry customer expects this. *They expect a fight from you.* They get it everywhere else when they have a bad buying experience, so why would dealing with you be any different?

Because you're a *professional*. And you've mastered the third Success Skill of Professional Salespeople: paraphrasing.

Paraphrasing for needs analysis and solving customer disputes

While we focused earlier in the book on paraphrasing during the sales process, paraphrasing is also great for many different forms of communication. Now you're using it to fully understand the depth of your customer's dissatisfaction based on the *words they use and the feelings they express.* Great paraphrasing shows you are actively listening and that you *get it.* It can have a tremendous ability to calm highly charged, emotional customers.

After paraphrasing them, ask them this question:

"Am I on the right track? Have I left anything out?"

Wait for the *"No."* They may have the look of *"So, what you are going to do about it?"* They are now ready for interaction.

Step #3 – Offer a deserved explanation, not an excuse

Here's your next message to your customer:

"I think you deserve an explanation for what happened. I'm really going to try to ensure that this doesn't sound like an excuse to you. I know you're unhappy. I just want you to know why this happened."

As you give them the real explanation, consider their emotions and watch for a rebuttal. Take their argument away by saying:

"I know what you're thinking – How is that my problem? Right? (pause) It's not. It's simply an explanation of what happened."

Watch for the nod

You just turned their desire to argue with you into agreement. Man, you're good! You could defuse bombs for a living! Now, let's move ahead . . .

Step #4 – Move together toward a solution

Here's your next question:

"Can we work together to solve this issue?" (Wait for a *"Yes"* or some sign of acceptance.)

This is such a powerful statement. Here's what you are really saying:

"I understand. You're beyond annoyed. I get it. You want to be treated like you should've been in the first place. Can we move past that now, so we can actually do something about it?"

Hilarious

Naturally, you wouldn't get away with saying that. Not for a second! Yet asking your customer for permission to work together to solve the problem does *exactly that!* That's why Professional Salespeople earn great incomes. They are masters of communication.

You should now have a very clear picture of what the issue is, why the customer is upset and how you might be able to work together to solve the problem and turn this bad experience into a good one. There's just one final step – *and please don't skip it*!

Step #5 – Ask for closure

This final step is so easy yet so important. It gives you the opportunity to see the results of your patience and hard work. After you've proposed and discussed your solution, ask this question:

"Do you feel we have managed to solve the problem today?" (Wait for the answer.)

"Is there anything that is still unresolved?" (Wait for the answer.)

Once again, here's your message...

"OK, so can we close the book on this issue and not have to deal with it again? It's 100% totally finished with? Is that what we're agreeing to here?"

When you have the power to deliver strong messages like this with great tact and diplomacy, it makes your job as a Professional Salesperson enjoyable. Maybe even fun. Here's another great point on asking for closure:

Your unhappy customer may become the president of your fan club

 This customer who was unhappy and ready to personally drive your company into bankruptcy is now so impressed with your tact that she's become a *powerful advocate*. She might even be one of your most influential salespeople on the street simply because of the unexpectedly positive way by which you resolved the problem.

People like to tell others about their unexpected customer experiences – *good or bad*. By addressing the negative experience and replacing it in your customer's memory with a positive one, you're opening yourself up to referrals as the story of your professional, proactive resolution starts to spread.

Whether this happens through word of mouth or word of keyboard, it's all the same to your reputation.

 A bad experience doesn't create the final customer experience. It's how you deal with it that does!

CHAPTER 32
How to Get and Use Great Client Testimonials

Professional Salespeople know the power of great client testimonials. A few great testimonials can add tremendous credibility to you, your products and your services. So why are they so difficult to get?

For years, I would ask each of my best clients for a written testimonial. Though every one of them would agree, weeks would go by without hearing back from them.

Easy to agree to – tough to deliver

In their defence, your customers, like mine, are busy people with too much to do and too little time to do it. I'm also willing to bet that many of your best clients do not consider themselves great writers. Just the thought of writing a testimonial causes them to procrastinate.

There is, however, a sure-fire way to get something that's even better than a written testimonial. It's creative, painless and incredibly effective. Better yet, it's *easy* to get.

Your personal testimonial page

Any time a client gives you or your company a verbal compliment, ask them this question:

"Would you mind if I used those words on my testimonial page? Chances are, they'll ask:

What's a testimonial page?

A testimonial page is a simple idea that sends a strong message of recommendation. It's a one-page document that's creative and colourful, with highlights and flattering comments that your clients have made to you verbally. Anyone with some experience in graphic design and a decent computer can create one for you.

Perhaps you read the great professional testimonials about this book. Thank you to my colleagues for being so kind! Words of commendation are always powerful influencers.

Your testimonial page addresses your *character* as a Professional Salesperson. It could include comments like these:

"In my five years of working with Michael, he has always exceeded my expectations."

"Amanda is hard-working and resourceful. She brings dignity to her profession."

"Mark has been our trusted advisor for the past 10 years. His opinion is based on my needs – always. I know he would never suggest anything to me unless he truly believed in it."

Powerful statements

These mini-testimonials are followed by the person's name, title and company. Be smart and include an image of them. Either ask them for a professional business photo or just ask to take a quick picture with your smartphone.

Why this works so well

Your clients are busy. They are probably not authors. Many struggle with the right words to use. Just the effort alone in writing the testimonial may discourage them from even starting. By you seizing the opportunity when your clients compliment you, you *fast track* the process.

No waiting for them to write it. No reminding them to do it. No delicate conversations about spelling and grammatical mistakes. You get what you want immediately – a powerful, short, effective testimonial that could influence other key decision-makers.

Or hire a professional

Another great way to get testimonials is to hire a third party, especially someone with great writing skills, to solicit them for you. The advantage of this method is that it enables you to get punchy, effective testimonials while avoiding the awkwardness of asking for a glowing review of yourself or prodding your clients to expand on just how great they think you are.

Here's how it can work effectively:

1. You give your best clients a heads-up that you're putting together some testimonials and ask their permission for someone to contact them for feedback. No one who sincerely enjoys doing business with you will object.

2. Your writer then makes a five-minute call to each client and drafts a testimonial based on that conversation. The beauty here is that the writer can lead the conversation down different alleys based on your guidance. For example, if one client really appreciated your flexibility, the writer can ask about that. A long-time client can be asked what makes her keep doing business with you. A skilled interviewer will delve deeper than the initial platitudes and clichés and get a real gem has true meaning as a testimonial. The writer can also paraphrase or even put words in your clients' mouths when the sentiment is there but the words just aren't flowing.

3. This is the key part – the writer then sends a draft of the testimonial to each client via email for their approval. Very seldom do clients make substantial changes to their testimonial.

4. The writer sends you the approved testimonials, each one direct, to the point and utterly glowing with praise for you and your impeccable service. Instead of a bunch of generic testimonials that offer no real substance, you get several distinct ones that each focus on a different benefit of working with you. They're short, punchy and incredibly powerful.

The comparison

When you buy a product or service online, you look for positive reviews;

they serve as a powerful endorsement that you're making the right decision. Your personal testimonial page does *exactly that* when decision-makers are searching for your product or service. If you wish to be a leader in your field, have the philosophy of *Go Big or Go Home*. Customers want to buy from someone who they consider to be an expert.

A client testimonial page has many uses!

 It can be included in proposals or PowerPoint presentations. Professional Salespeople pass it to potential customers who are considering a purchase to show their credibility and professionalism. Make sure it's available through your personal website, and also ensure you have printed copies on hand to offer clients.

Continue to leverage it

Keep your testimonial page handy on your computer desktop so you can send it via email whenever appropriate. Freely offering your testimonial sheet shows you have confidence in what you have to offer – and that's attractive to buyers.

CHAPTER 33
How to Deal with the Lower Price Competitor

The top Professional Salespeople believe in offering their clients extraordinary service – beyond what's expected of them. These Sales Superstars feel that a significant part of buying their product is the service their customers receive from them. They don't get worried when another supplier offers a similar product for less money.

Once you incorporate the following strategies into your own career, you won't either.

Two pricing models

 In every industry, in every market, there will be two suppliers on direct opposite ends of the price spectrum. There will likely also be a few more somewhere in the middle. Both the high-priced supplier and the low-priced supplier will claim to have a competitive advantage based on value. It's the *interpretation* of that value that will make the difference.

The higher price model

This supplier believes in offering a product whose exceptionally high quality *exceeds* that of the competition. This company employs great salespeople and other team members who believe in consistently offering exceptional levels of customer service.

Companies on the high end have the confidence to *charge accordingly* and will knowingly tell their clients that they don't offer the lowest price. They offer value based on the premise that *you get what you pay for*. They tend to have close relationships with their buyers, with service and expertise being a major part of the client experience.

The lower price model

These suppliers decide to go the other way. They may still have a decent product with fair levels of service, yet not to the same degree as their high-end competitors. Their competitive advantage is price. They claim to offer value in having the *lowest price*, knowing the sensitivity of cost to all buyers.

Here's the challenge

As a Professional Salesperson representing the company with the higher price model, you work diligently to ensure your clients are happy. You treat them with respect and consistently over-deliver. You not only do everything your clients expect, you go the extra mile and ensure that they never question their business with you. Until one day you receive the call . . .

 "I'm starting to question your prices," your client says. It appears a salesperson from the lower price model supplier has caused this client to take a second look at your competitor based *solely* on price. Remember that you have no justification to get upset over another salesperson doing her job, or a client doing his due diligence.

What do you do?

Schedule a meeting with your client. Don't tackle such an important issue on the phone, where you can't read your client's body language and reaction. Ask them what's recently occurred to cause them to question price. Don't start mud-slinging. Show the class you're known for and take the high road.

Ask them if they're happy with your product. How about your service? They will tell you that they love doing business with you on both counts. It's *price* that's the issue. Fight the urge to reduce price. That's a slippery slope that will require you to reduce price every time the issue comes up in the future. *Don't train your clients to expect this.*

Consider that your client may actually want to keep doing business with you. They may be trying to *leverage* an offer from another supplier to their advantage. That's their job. It's your job to attempt to stick to your price.

My suggested response:

"I understand. We all want to get the best product and service for the lowest price. (Name), I can't control what my competition does. Our business, your business and even our competitor's business sets its prices based on supply, demand and value. I'm sure they have a decent product and fair service. I don't know why they sell it for less.

"(Name), let me ask you this question: If they could charge more for their product, do you think they would? Our customers deal with us because they get a great product and my personal service for a price that offers true value. Does that seem reasonable?"

Now shut up and wait for their response. The first one who talks loses.

Offer something

If possible, offer something of value to your client as a gesture of appreciation for their business. Try to avoid a price reduction. And no, don't just give them a free pen. Try to offer something that costs your company very little yet has high perceived value. Car dealerships do this extremely well with no charge customized mats, service appointments and vouchers for free fuel.

How can you prevent this from happening in the future?

The best time to fight a price objection is *before it occurs*. It's your job as a Professional Salesperson to build up the value of what you have to offer, and then take away the price objection by having a frank discussion about it. That will prepare your client to accept that you are representing a high-end supplier. It also takes away the objection *later* when the lower price model salesperson comes calling.

One more point

When you're giving your client the extraordinary service that you're known for, find a tactful way to remind them of the commitment you make to the relationship.

Take your choice from these statements:

1. *"I'm really happy to give you the level of service you deserve."*

2. *"All of my best clients get my best service."*

3. *"It's really important to me that you're pleased with my service."*

Internalize one (or more) of them and make it yours. Consider giving your clients a quarterly summary of the value-add services you've been happy to provide to them at no additional cost. When I've done this before, some client's have actually asked me if I intend to invoice them on this. *"No, of course not, I just wanted you to have a summary of what I'm doing for you above and beyond at no-cost."*

Don't you love it when a plan comes together?

Is this beating your own chest?

It sure is. This is one instance where it's in your interest to do so. You're not being a sales ape and beating your chest trying to win a sale – you're simply reminding your clients why they enjoy doing business with you. *They will forget unless you keep them educated.*

Don't miss this step and allow your clients to take your high level of service for granted. They seldom ever get your level of service from the low-cost provider.

CHAPTER 34
Win-Win Negotiating

Negotiating can be one of the toughest skills for salespeople to master. At the start of my sales career, I hated negotiating because I didn't think I was good at it. Big surprise. *How often are you good at something you dislike?*

Today, however, I love negotiating. I genuinely enjoy the process because I've become really good at it. You can too.

This is common

 As an inexperienced salesperson, I used to bring every deal that required negotiating to my sales manager. I felt that was his job. After all, that's why they paid him the big bucks, wasn't it? My job was to represent my client's best interests and bring in all offers. Sound familiar?

This is the sign of someone who doesn't like negotiating.

My sales manager

 This guy was, and still is, unbelievable. The tougher the negotiation, the more he enjoyed it. He actually smiled and was genuinely amused throughout the process. He always seemed to get a much better deal than *I ever could.* He seldom lost a client by negotiating and managed to get virtually every client to move toward concessions.

One day, after a particularly impressive negotiation, I shook my head in disbelief and told him that I'd never be able to do what he does. He laughed and said one simple thing: "*If you want to learn how to be great at it, you will.*"

Enough said. He knew I would accept the challenge and how to motivate me. That's the sign of a great leader.

Win-win negotiating

 Don't be misled. The key to proper negotiating is *not* getting the best of the other party. It's not your job to railroad them, trick them or put them over a barrel. That's win-*lose* negotiating. Win-lose negotiating will win you clients who are more critical of your services in the midst of a long-term agreement. The relationship is devoid of trust and respect.

 Win-win negotiating is finalizing a deal that is fair enough for both parties in meeting their needs and creating a good working relationship for the future.

Win-win negotiating sees *both* parties make concessions to accept a common agreement to move ahead. Notice I said parties, not *sides*. Negotiating should not be a battle. Everyone involved needs to win in order to foster a professional relationship that will lead to repeat business and referrals.

Win-win negotiating shows respect for both parties and the willingness to ensure the other party is, at the very least, *satisfied* – if not excited about the outcome.

Five negotiation misconceptions

Why are so many of us uncomfortable with negotiating? Why do so few negotiators seek out a win-win and instead try to secure the best deal possible for themselves? It may have something do with five huge misconceptions about negotiating.

Misconception #1: Good negotiators are born

 There's no negotiating gene. I'll concede that negotiating skills can be *taught* at a very young age, but no one is born a good negotiator.

Misconception #2: Experience is a good teacher

 Possibly, if the experience has been good. If your past attempts have been unsuccessful, you've probably learned to negotiate poorly. You need to learn how to negotiate based on a successful strategy.

Misconception #3: Good negotiators take risks

 Not so. They determine the power of their position and estimate what the other party's strengths and desires might be. Smart salespeople plan their negotiation far in advance with research and mental role-playing. They reduce risk by *doing their homework.*

Misconception #4: Good negotiators rely on intuition

 Only after they've fully done #3. *Intuition is not a replacement for preparation.* Good negotiators will use intuition after doing their due diligence.

Misconception #5: Good negotiators use ultimatums

 Not at all. Poor negotiators give you the give-me-what-I-want-or-I'll-walk feeling. There's another word for people like that. Bullies.

The five fatal mistakes of negotiating

 Just as there are five common misconceptions about negotiating, so are there five fatal mistakes that far too many salespeople make when negotiating.

1. Leaving money on the table
Ouch! They agreed too fast. I wonder what you could have

negotiated if you'd asked for more?

2. Settling for too little

Giving up too early on concessions. You negotiated the deal, yet don't feel good about the terms of the agreement. You ended up making concessions that you really didn't want to make, and you're not happy with the deal.

3. Getting too much

OK, that was strange. Why did the other party give up so easily? I sense remorse or payback coming. . . .

4. Walking away from the table

What the heck just happened? Is this really what everyone wanted? This occurs when you don't prepare well and let emotions control your decisions. Now you have to figure out how to bring the deal back to life – no easy task.

5. Settling for worse terms than your current position (or cost of acquisition)

Your customer smelled your desperation in getting a deal done. You've now decided to go backwards and don't even want to talk about it. You'd rather take the business, run and forget the details. This also occurs when you don't prepare and move too fast.

Your three positions

There are three vital positions with which you need to enter every negotiation.

A successful negotiation will be completed with the two of you meeting in the middle somewhere. To do this, both of you will be coming from opposite directions and making concessions step-by-step in good faith. Unless, of course, you're not prepared. Fail to identify your three positions heading in and the other party will take you for a walk around the block on a leash like a good puppy. Admit it – you've had that happen before, haven't you?

1. Your target position

This is your first offer. It's the deal you would *love*, yet don't expect the other party to agree to. If they do, take care of them and over-deliver as much as you can. You know that neither party is likely to accept the initial offer, yet you also know you have to start with your target in order to establish a starting position, called the anchor. We'll get to that in a moment.

2. Your fall back position

This is your second offer. It's the deal you would *like to sign and be OK with*. It's the deal you really expect to make. Remember, ultimatums are delivered by poor negotiators, not good ones. Your fall back position acknowledges that you're *willing to make concessions.*

3. Your line in the sand

This is the deal you'll *live with – nothing less*. Anything below the line in the sand is worth *walking away* from, as the pain of the deal is greater than the reward, regardless of terms. Most of us have accepted a deal like this before. We accept them for many reasons, some of the most common being client history, payment terms, multi-platform purchases and breaking into a new business category. If you're entering a negotiation that fits any of those descriptions, be very conscious of your line in the sand.

Heads Up! Set your positions in advance

Set up your target, fall back and line in the sand *before* you start negotiating. Don't allow emotions to cloud your judgment during the exchange. You will not think clearly about setting or adjusting these positions after you start.

The anchor

The anchor is *the initial reference point* that acts as a comparison throughout the negotiation. Note that it doesn't have to be solely a price – it can also include extra features and additional terms. In virtually all cases, your anchor should be *your target position – the deal you'd love*! The other party will want to establish their own anchor marking their target position – the deal *they* would love!

Understand the big picture

 As you are setting your three positions – target (anchor), fall back and line in the sand – the other party is doing the same thing! Your target positions will likely be far apart, and your fall back positions will be getting closer. The key to completing a win-win negotiation lies in your respective lines in the sand.

If the two lines in the sand are still apart, you will not have a deal.

The four lessons of win-win negotiating

There are four major lessons to learn about negotiating. Each of them is crucial. Let them be your guiding principles for establishing win-win agreements.

Lesson 1: Slow down – speed kills

 Speed is always on the side of the buyer. Your client has had time to prepare and is calling you with a super-quick deadline to make a purchase. This gives you little to no time to prepare for the negotiation. Have you ever heard something like this?

"Look, I thought I would give you the opportunity for the business. We're close to making a final decision and if you want to be considered, give us your best offer right up front. There won't be any time for a second round, so sharpen your pencil and get back to us as quickly as possible before we make our final choice."

I bet this has even happened to you: after the buyer plays the *"speed card"* and you make a lowball offer (hoping your sales manager will forgive you), the buyer suddenly seems to have all the time in the world to get back to you. You've just been played by a professional negotiator.

So what *should* you do?

Ask for more time. What's the worst they can say, no? You miss 100% of the shots you don't take. Any extension you receive will slow down the speed of the negotiation. One more time: s*peed is always on the side of the buyer.*

If your client does say no and won't give you additional time, then you *need* to start with your target position. This is where inexperienced salespeople shake in their boots in fear of losing the deal by not ignoring what the client said about leading with the best price. You heard them all right – just stay calm, smile and lay your anchor.

Heads Up! Don't panic

Don't *ever* lower your price before the negotiation starts. If you do, here's what your negotiating partner is thinking:

"I haven't even started to negotiate and already they've dropped their price! This should be fun . . . "

Lesson 2: Practise due diligence

If this is a renewal of an agreement, do all of your research on the last deal *before* starting the negotiation. Look at everything offered in the last deal, plus all the value-add components you threw in for no charge throughout the term. Consider all the components added together. *Assume the other party is doing the same.*

Lesson 3: Assess the other's position

This one, like the first two, needs to take place *before* the negotiation begins. What issues will be important to the other party? What will be on their wish list? What could they ask for, yet concede as a bargaining chip? Consider their strengths and weaknesses in their approach with you. How will you counter their concerns?

Lesson 4: Follow a strategy

There is a true science to the art of negotiation. *"Winging it"* and seeing what happens is foolish. A pre-determined plan of offers and concessions will give you a systematic framework for proper negotiation. Do your homework and enter the negotiation with your three positions firmly in mind. Stick to your guns.

Experts of negotiation have internalized these lessons and use these four techniques from the boardrooms of multinational corporations to the trinket vendors on the beaches of Mexico. You're going to love this!

Heads Up! Always get a concession for every one you make!

In many negotiations, the other party will be direct and possibly even emotional. You might hear something like this:

"I'm not paying that price! I don't care what other clients pay, didn't you hear what I said last time?"

In this case you may have to move away from your target position quickly. Just make sure you get something in return, like a long-term commitment, higher quantity order, etc.

The law of reciprocity

Every time you make a concession, *ask for one back.* That applies whether it's a price concession or a value-add. If you don't, you'll soon discover that, while you were making concessions, an experienced negotiator has attached a leash to your collar and is heading out the door to take you for a walk.

Have confidence in the value of your product or service and *hold your ground*. If the buyer wasn't interested, they wouldn't have engaged you in the process up until now.

Heads Up! Don't skip any steps

Don't skip or fast track your negotiating positions to drive for a quick resolution. That's what your negotiating partner wants – *a quick end*. A client of mine once gave me this gem:

"Don't screw this up kid, this is the easiest renewal you've ever had."

That client taught me more about negotiating than any book ever could. Slow the process down, ask questions, smile and enjoy the opportunity to negotiate. The better you get at it, the more fun it will be.

Heads Up! Too much information

Don't ever reveal your line in the sand position. If you do, your negotiating partner is sure to go there for a quick close – *if they believe you.* Experienced negotiators will bluff you on their line in the sand. If they think you're doing the same, they may try to low-ball you into accepting a weaker deal.

The ultimate client challenge we've all heard before:

"Your competition is willing to sell me exactly the same thing for less than you."

The best thing you could say back:

Even though this was mentioned in a previous chapter, it's worth repeating.

"I understand. We all want to get the best product and service for the lowest price. (Name), I can't control what my competition does. Our business, your business and even

our competitor's business sets its prices based on supply, demand and value. I'm sure they have a decent product and fair service. I don't know why they sell it for less.

"(Name), let me ask you this question: If they could charge more for their product, do you think they would? Our customers deal with us because they get a great product and my personal service for a price that offers true value. Does that seem reasonable?"

Now shut up, look them in the eye and wait for their response. The first one who talks loses.

You will either get the deal or a renewed sense of pride. Every time I deliver that line with passion and conviction, I get *a smile* from the other party. Some clients have even said to me, *"I wish I had more salespeople like you."*

My reply? *"I wish I had more clients like you."*

That's why Professional Salespeople have the potential to make incredible incomes. We relate to people, tell great stories and have confidence in what we have to offer. We're proud people. Hopefully, not too proud.

The late Casey Kasem had a trademark phrase that is fitting.

"Keep your feet on the ground and keep reaching for the stars."

CHAPTER 35
Confidence is Good. Ego is Bad

There is a fine line between *confidence* and *ego*. Ego is a widespread business problem that accounts for office gossip, lost productivity, frustration and, in severe cases, the decision to move on to another opportunity. *A healthy confidence level can lead to an inflated ego.*

Every one of us who has accomplished something of merit in life has an ego. Understand the parameters of yours. Know when your ego is creeping over your self confidence. Be careful of mistaking one for the other.

What's the difference between the two?

I'm sure you have at least one person in your office who suffers from an overly inflated ego. Hopefully, you're also surrounded by people with healthy self-confidence. Before we go any further, here's how I differentiate between the two:

Ego: An exaggerated sense of self-importance; conceit, arrogance.

Self-confidence: Confidence in oneself and one's abilities.

Similarities

Both ego and self-confidence are qualities capable of influencing opinion and drawing attention to the individual. Both ego and self-confidence can be found within leaders and are powerful components of their ability and personal style. Here are three examples. In each case, ask yourself – *Is this an example of self confidence or ego?*

- Donald Trump when he uses the infamous words *"You're fired!"*

- The late Steve Jobs was known to have a fiery temper and being hard to please.

- Warren Buffet, one of the world's most respected investors, pulls a mere salary of $100,000 and still thinks that steak, Cherry Coke and DQ ice cream is a great meal.

Differences

 Ego tends to have a negative connotation. Too much ego can drive you to take actions you really shouldn't, such as:

- *You stop doing the things that made you successful because you feel you shouldn't have to anymore.*

- *Your primary motivations to do anything are praise and recognition.*

- *You become openly defensive and are seldom open-minded to opinions that differ from yours.*

- *You constantly compare yourself to others in an effort to always one-up them.*

- *You call the shots openly and strive to be in control at all times.*

 Self-confidence, on the other hand, is a positive attribute. It allows you to take steps that are beneficial to your career, such as:

- *You continue to do the things that made you successful to stay grounded and keep you real.*

- *You are encouraged to praise and recognize other people to share their success.*

- *Your ability to stay open-minded and listen to all opinions encourages people to participate.*

- *You are known to put yourself at the back of the line, allowing others to go first.*

- *Your self-confidence leads to respect, trust and admiration from co-workers and clients.*

My personal observation

People who have an inflated ego can suffer from low self-confidence. Those with strong self-confidence have no need to assert their ego. There will be moments for all of us to observe our actions and ask this question.

"Is this my self-confidence speaking, or my ego overtaking my actions?"

CHAPTER 36
The Power of Social Media for Professional Salespeople

Every salesperson has an opinion about social media and how it should (or shouldn't) be used in sales. Veteran salespeople are often heard making comments like these:

"There has never been, and never will be, a replacement for the face-to-face meeting."

"I would like to see these so-called social media experts prove to me that all this stuff actually results in sales made. Show me the money!"

"Too many Salespeople look for shortcuts to building relationships. Get on the phone, make appointments and get out and shake some hands. That's what sales is about!"

"Young people don't even know how to have a conversation anymore. Put your phone away, look up and talk to me!"

Are you nodding your head in agreement? If so, I encourage you to keep an open mind as you read the following chapters. Give some of these techniques a try. I think you'll be surprised by how effective social media can be when used appropriately.

The new generation of salespeople may think:

"Those ways just don't work as well anymore. We live in a world of technology – why not embrace it?"

"Being successful in sales means adapting to new ways to do business."

"Didn't the creation of email allow salespeople to reach more people faster? Is this the next big thing?"

"Hey Grandpa, here's a calculator. You can put away the pencil."

Great arguments!

Well, maybe not the last one. The topic of social media always sparks a lively discussion in sales meetings and on the sales floor. Like most arguments with vigorous support on both sides, no one side is completely right – or wrong.

Here's my take

There is no replacement for a face-to-face meeting. Social media can help you get a qualified prospect.

Social media is another creative way to reach people. It can also be a very effective one. The ABCs of sales have changed from *Always Be Closing* to *Always Be Connecting.* Connecting with existing clients about their changing needs, connecting with new potential customers and connecting to establish relationships that turn into future sales.

Here's my caveat. Call it a nod to those old-school veteran salespeople. *Many of us are addicted to technology and need to unplug occasionally.* For the record, I am not the best example in this regard. At times, I catch myself (OK, my wife catches me.) There's a time and a place for everything. All the time, everywhere is not a fitting example for social media.

My experience

My company, **PROSALESGUY TRAINING Inc.**, is kept very busy with inbound potential clients. Approximately 50% of our business comes from referrals and past relationships. The remaining 50% of business comes equally from the contact form on our website and my LinkedIn Profile. LinkedIn is an excellent way of reaching business-to-business decision makers.

In the upcoming chapter on LinkedIn, I will give you my recommendation of an expert who greatly influenced my personal LinkedIn profile.

Will the proper use of social media result in sales?

 Yes. Of that, I have no doubt. Notice my choice of words: *proper use*. We'll get into that shortly. I'd like to personally attest that social media has brought me buyers from previously non-existent relationships. People *I didn't know* before social media are now my clients.

Now a warning: beware the temptation to over-rely on social media! You may be enticed to think that cold calling is dead given all the hype generated by social media and its claims. *It's not.*

We're always attracted to the shiny new toy of technology. Too many salespeople look for shortcuts. Social media should be added to proven methods of prospecting for new business. Don't abandon what works to *try something else* that works! Combine your efforts.

Look at it this way

 Wouldn't it be smart to combine everything that works in sales into one cohesive strategy? Can we not stand on the shoulders of decades of proven experience while also staying open-minded to new techniques? That's just smart business.

You as your own business

Social media enables professional salespeople to *market* themselves. Your company is attempting to convince buyers to purchase its products and services through positioning in the marketplace. You should be doing the same to entice buyers to buy from *you* specifically. Customers should be asking for *you* when they call or walk into your store, emailing *you* directly about your product and service and reaching out to *you* on social media.

Wouldn't that put more money in your pocket?

Wouldn't it be a change of pace to have clients pursuing you?

Don't allow your commission paycheque to be influenced solely by the advertising and marketing that your company does or doesn't do. Take matters into your own hands. Be proactive. *Market yourself.*

Things salespeople say:

"If our company would spend more on advertising, we'd have more traffic and make more sales."

"Why is our company spending so much money on (this form of advertising) and not using (another form of advertising)?"

"I don't like the commercial we have. I think it could have been a lot better."

Stop complaining and do something about it. Give people a reason to seek you out and want to do business with you. Run your client base like a business within the structure of the company you work for. Control your destiny.

Search engine optimization (SEO)

I'm a firm believer that every Professional Salesperson should learn a little bit about search engine optimization (SEO). Although the specifics of SEO are beyond the scope of this book, there are lots of great resources online and at your local library or bookstore.

Social media will strengthen your SEO and help steer buyers in your direction. It will help you establish your reputation as an authority in your field. *All buyers want to deal with someone they regard as a leader in their field.* It feels good to be important enough to be in the hands of an expert.

By using social media and being conscious of how you can improve your search engine visibility, you can create an expectation of great service, knowledge and expertise. You can cultivate a great reputation with buyers who have never even met you.

Now that's cool.

What's your digital footprint?

I learned this technique from a Professional Salesperson that I admire and respect. He advises business owners and decision-makers on how to drive revenues through online awareness and positioning. First, he assesses a company's current *digital footprint* by placing specific keywords and phrases into Google. Then he makes recommendations of how they can improve their ranking.

 When I went on some clients calls with him, hearing his term *digital footprint* was a eureka moment for me.

Every Professional Salesperson should be doing this!

It's easy

Plug your name into Google. What comes up?

Nothing? Eight other people with the same name as you? Your Facebook page? Your name listed as part of a local community group? Your picture in the online version of your local newspaper? All of these form part of your digital footprint. It's the part that occurs by *default* not *design*.

As a Professional Salesperson, wouldn't you rather *these* showed up?

Your LinkedIn Profile.

Your Twitter and Google+ profile.

An online article recognizing you for an award you won or accomplishment you achieved.

Professional comments that you made on someone's industry blog post.

These links can be powerful resources that sway people toward wanting to deal with you when looking for your product or service.

I'm not suggesting that everyone looking to buy your product or service is going to Google your name to check you out first. I'm merely pointing out that the better your reputation, the more people will *gravitate toward you*. Social media didn't create that – it's common sense. Social media fuels it by creating the perception that you are an *expert* and a *leader in your field*.

Social media best practices

To get the best returns from social media and blogging, Professional Salespeople need to be diligent with its use. As you read through the following chapters on the various social media applications and how to best take advantage of them, keep the following guidelines in mind:

- Many countries have anti-spam laws in place, with Canada's recent legislation regarded as stringent with many wide-ranging provisions and huge penalties. Check the laws in the country you are communicating with to ensure you are being legally compliant with practices.

- *Always ensure your profile is 100% complete.* Getting it to that level gives you the best opportunity for leverage and success.

- *Capitalize on Influence.* This is a measure of your activity. How well are you fuelling social media to get noticed? *What are you doing to encourage people to reach out to you?*

- *Be active with engagement.* How proactive are you in reaching out to people on social media? Comment on their blogs, tweets, posts and influence efforts. Social media success comes faster when you practise a good balance of posting your own content and commenting on content posted by others.

- *Pick one form of social media and make it successful.* Baby steps. Rome wasn't built in a day. Select the social media application that makes the most sense based on you as a Professional Salesperson, your products and services. Make a time commitment that you can honour. *Don't start the second platform until you feel you've done the first one justice.* It's better to do a great job with one form of social media than a mediocre job with two.

Social media can be incredibly powerful and can greatly contribute to your success as a Professional Salesperson. For it to work, though, you need to work it.

Allow me to help!

 I will always have the most up-to-date information and social media tips on **THE PROSALESGUY BLOG** and its archives at **www.prosalesguy.ca**. Social media is always changing and adapting to the needs of its users. My blog will give you details on trends and new ways to reach out to new potential clients by creating inbound marketing.

I always welcome your comments on your personal experiences with social media. Have you made a sales breakthrough by using social media? Have you had a great or not-so-great social media experience? Either way, please email me at **dave@prosalesguy.ca**. I always make a commitment to respond to everyone who takes the time to reach out. That's how we all learn – together.

CHAPTER 37
How to Use Facebook and Google+

Facebook is the granddaddy and largest social media application. It's, by far, the most common form of social media that most people are using. Currently, 48% of all Facebook users log on daily and spend an average of 18 minutes per visit. Each day, Facebook records nearly 15,000 hours of usage. *That's almost two years of time spent on Facebook every day!*

Founded in 2004, its widespread use has kept many of us in touch with family and friends and caused many more of us to become inexplicably addicted to creating fantasy farms. As a Professional Salesperson, imagine using Facebook for professional purposes.

Your fan page

Facebook distinguishes between a *profile* – the personal page with which most of us are most familiar – and a *page* – a different kind of profile that followers choose to *like* rather than *friend*. Facebook created these pages for companies and organizations to reach out to their *fans*.

A Facebook fan page is great for B2C – Business to Consumer companies. It's an extension of your brand and encourages people to show their preference for you by *"liking"* the page. A business can use its fan page to keep in touch with its core supporters, educate consumers on its new products or services and create buying incentives – and much more!

While B2B – Business to Business companies may also have a fan page, in my opinion there are other, better-suited social media options for this category.

Facebook suggestions

If you're a Professional Salesperson with a B2C company, your company may already have a Facebook fan page. If not, encourage your boss to set one up. It allows great opportunities for customer engagement and can definitely drive traffic to your location.

Professional Salespeople can also get creative with their personal Facebook profile. Every so often, take a picture of you doing something creative on the job.

"Look, I just sold a new (product or service) to our mayor! Cool!"

What this does is ensure that all of your contacts are aware of what you do for a living. It's not pushy or intrusive, but it might encourage them to seek you out should they wish to buy.

Stop! PROPER USE!

Remember what I said about *proper use* of social media? Don't turn into a sales ape and start beating your chest, spewing unsolicited propaganda and using your Facebook soapbox as a way to annoy innocent people. That's a sure-fire way to lose friends on Facebook and in real life.

Use common sense and remember that the rules of social etiquette apply everywhere. Don't take a picture of yourself and everyone you sold something to and slap it on your Facebook Page, and don't use Facebook *only* for advertising your products and services. There's a reason it's called *"social"* media. Being obnoxious is not the way to win friends and influence people. *Don't be a jerk!*

Look for content that is worthy and that you think your followers will genuinely enjoy or otherwise appreciate.

Google+

Created in 2011, Google+ is consistently gaining in popularity. It may not be as popular (yet) as Facebook, Twitter or LinkedIn, but you can expect that to change quickly, as it continues to attract new users at a rapid rate. Keep in mind that less users means less competition to get noticed with a predominately business user crowd. The name says it all: Google+ will most definitely be a focus for Google in its release of future products.

Circles and hangouts

Google+ enables you to add people to your *circles*. For example, you might have one circle for school friends, one for business associates and another for family. If you want more people in your circles, lead by example and add the types of people you're looking to attract.

A related tool, *Google+ Hangouts*, also allows you to hold video discussions with the people in your circles. Think about ways you can use this tool creatively, such as by hosting a webinar or product demonstration. If nothing else, social media is a forum for creativity and expression.

If your company isn't yet using Google+, try to entice your boss to establish a business profile with your geographic location to make use of the great features of Google+.

The greatest advantage to Google+

 Cultivating your profile on Google+ carries many of the same benefits as it does on Facebook. Google+ also gives you another huge advantage, and it's right there in its name. *Google*. Heard of them?

If you have a Google+ Profile and post great content, it contributes in a big way to your personal SEO as a Professional Salesperson. Google is a smart company. The algorithm that it uses to create ranking order in organic searches is greatly influenced by its many corollary applications – like Google+. Leverage those applications to your advantage.

Posting

Professional Salespeople can very easily post links to articles and blogs on Google+. The same rule that I mentioned about Facebook, however, also applies here: Don't inundate the people in your circles with propaganda! Instead, deliver *great content* that will inform, entertain or otherwise please your potential customers. Be a resource for knowledge and education. Establish yourself as an expert. Be memorable for the right reasons.

CHAPTER 38
How to Use LinkedIn

 LinkedIn is one my favourite social media applications and I spend the most time on it. It can be very effective when used to its potential. *LinkedIn is like Facebook for business people.*

LinkedIn provides the perfect online venue for you to deliver on the ABCs of Sales – *Always be Connecting*. It's like going to a social networking event, except you get to connect with so many more people because *this event never ends*. It goes on 24/7, giving you the opportunity to establish great online relationships with people you likely never would have met otherwise.

And as we know, strong relationships are key to building your business.

A brief history of LinkedIn

When LinkedIn launched in 2003, it had an immediate business benefit based on its premise. From the start, it was fertile ground to be used as an employment tool. People looking for work and recruiters looking for talent suddenly had an easy, effective way to quickly connect online. While that function still exists today, LinkedIn's subscribers know that it offers professionals so much more. More to the point, LinkedIn offers *huge* networking benefits to Professional Salespeople.

LinkedIn applications for business

LinkedIn is a B2B – Business to Business – *powerhouse*. It's great for business owners, decision-makers and Professional Salespeople who want to stay connected with people they already know. More importantly, it's also a great way to initiate relationships with people you would *like* to know. Simply send a request to someone with whom you'd like to connect and wait for them to accept your invitation. Likewise, you'll receive requests from people who are reaching out to *you*. Some of them will be potential customers that you've never met face-to-face.

Not getting anywhere with a client because the decision-maker will not personally meet with you? Is your competitor so firmly entrenched with a client that you can't even get through the front door? LinkedIn may provide the key.

First, second and third-degree connections

Just like in real life, on LinkedIn you have the opportunity to be introduced to other people via a mutual connection. Simply look at the profile of one of your own acquaintances and scan their list of connections. The fewer people in the chain of connections between you and the person with whom you'd like to connect, the lower the degree of connection to you. Here's how it can work:

As you scan a colleague's connections, your eyes light up – *"Say, isn't that the regional marketing manager of that company that's opening a location in your community?"* She could be a great prospect for you as a Professional Media Salesperson. Suddenly you have an *"in"* through a mutual connection, and you may not have ever known about that connection otherwise. Now, instead of finding out that your colleague knows her after she's already designed and paid for her marketing campaign, you have an inside track to helping her launch the new location.

Introductions

LinkedIn also allows you to introduce yourself directly to potential new connections without an intermediary. Once again, it has some strong advantages over traditional networking. I certainly don't want to give the impression, however, that it should ever fully *replace* traditional networking. Nothing has the power of a *face-to-face meeting*.

How many times have you attended a business function and spotted a great potential connection from across the room? As you make your way to that person, however, you're continually sidetracked by all the people who want to say hello to you on the way. Even if you get there uninterrupted, that great person who you want to meet is in the midst of a conversation with someone else.

 This is one of the best features of LinkedIn – it allows you to quickly and easily connect with other professionals. It will even *suggest* people you may know. Want to find someone specific? Just enter their name into the search field at the top of the page. Easy.

A note about invitations

 I highly recommend that you do *not* send out the standard invitation that LinkedIn pre-writes for you. *Customize your message.* No sales propaganda like, "*I have an exciting new idea that I know will work well for you.*" *Salesperson Alert!* Sounds like a spammer, smells like a spammer – you will be labelled and marked as a spammer.

Being labelled as a spammer, of course, could seriously hamper your efforts to use LinkedIn properly. LinkedIn has specific rules and ways to protect the sincere nature of its platform. Have you ever seen a cyber-hooker with a LinkedIn profile? There's a very distinct reason for it. While Twitter allows a very broad list of subjects with a simple hashtag, LinkedIn preserves its forum for professional purposes.

Here's a much more powerful invitation:

 Mark, I spotted you at the (business function) last night and wanted to meet you. I thought I would send you an invitation to connect on LinkedIn. I look forward to having a chat soon. Thanks!

Almost every professional I know accepts invitations like this. Not accepting would be like walking away from someone who has extended his hand to meet you in person. That's just plain rude, and arrogant.

The next time you see Mark, he may actually make an effort to say hi. And even if he doesn't, you'll have an instant conversational ice-breaker:

Hi Mark! Thanks for accepting my invitation on LinkedIn. I see you at events like this often and have always wanted to meet you. It just never seems to work out. That's the great thing about LinkedIn. Do you find it useful in your business?

And off you go . . .

You're now expanding your network with a face-to-face exchange based on a social media connection. That's how you combine the best of both worlds.

Changes in decision-makers and work anniversaries on LinkedIn

Has one of your best buyers moved on to a new job? Would you like to be reminded when your clients are celebrating a work anniversary?

Staying up-to-date with the status changes of your clients is a consistent practice of Professional Salespeople. When your best buyer moves on to a new company, it creates two opportunities – one with her new company coupled with the need to find out who's replacing her to preserve the buying relationship with the current one.

LinkedIn shows you all of your contacts' work anniversaries and status changes and enables you to easily congratulate them when they find another employer. To be able to collect that kind of information without technology would be limited to your own individual efforts. That's an amazing benefit for Professional Salespeople!

Who's viewed your profile on LinkedIn

 Another feature of LinkedIn is the ability to see who's been looking at your profile. The information is available daily as it occurs and can be a gold mine.

Advanced Search feature on LinkedIn

LinkedIn's Advanced Search feature allows you to search its database by industry, job title, geographic location and more. *Imagine the power of that!*

Stop salivating

Slow down. Remember, you need to practise social media etiquette just as you would *social etiquette*. Don't be a spammer. Don't be a fox in the henhouse. LinkedIn will not allow you to run around on its site with a personal agenda of unsolicited selling. You will be caught and punished accordingly.

LinkedIn etiquette

Don't connect with everyone you can on LinkedIn to simply build connections and start spamming them.

Start relationships with businesspeople on LinkedIn based on establishing rapport and trust first.

Create a profile that attracts people to you and allows them to engage with you – not one that shoves propaganda down their throats.

Don't give people a reason to not want to meet and consider doing business with you.

Inbound opportunities

When a potential buyer reaches out to you, that's called an *inbound opportunity*. It sure is different than pursuing a dozen or more prospects to find someone interested in what you have to offer. Though LinkedIn facilitates this type of opportunity, that does not mean you should give up traditional, proven ways of establishing new business – like prospecting! *Add* to those efforts.

What would encourage someone to reach out to *you*?

At the risk of shameless self-promotion, visit my profile on LinkedIn.

Just go to LinkedIn.com and type in my name, "Dave Warawa." Click on my profile and check it out. It's packed with compelling information that makes decision-makers and fellow salespeople want to connect with me. Does your profile make people want to connect with *you*?

My personal recommendation

I have worked hard at my LinkedIn Profile. It brings me business. I highly recommend you check out the Profile of **Melonie Dodaro.** She's an expert on LinkedIn and has written a book called *"The LinkedIn Code."* Melonie can help you create the profile of an industry leader in your field. This kind of personal imaging creates the environment for in-bound marketing from qualified decision makers looking for experts in your field. I took one of her free webinars and applied every one of her recommendations.

Organic creativity

One of the things LinkedIn allows you to do is post links to YouTube videos, projects and people you've partnered with. Look at the videos I have on my LinkedIn profile. Did I spend a tonne of cash on a camera crew, editing, lighting and video production?

Not a chance. I bought a $70 high-definition webcam and a video editing program online. I shot the videos, posted them to YouTube (more on that later) and linked to them from LinkedIn. For my B2B business, LinkedIn is as important as my website. They complement and support one another.

Professional Salespeople understand that they also need to be Professional Marketers. The product is you. Why would I want to do business with you? What can you offer me? *What makes you different from everyone else?*

Creating your profile

When setting up your professional profile on LinkedIn, please take note of the word *professional*. Don't use your Facebook image, family picture or that photo of you with a big "P" painted on your chest at the football game. This is a branding opportunity, and first impressions count.

I'm not suggesting that your image needs to be formal and corporate. Choose something appropriate that makes sense based on your personality and occupation. If you'd like a professional photo, go for it, but it's not absolutely necessary. I've built professional profiles for individuals using a great shot from an iPhone.

Please also ensure you work toward reaching 100% profile completeness. LinkedIn will guide you along the way, making recommendations and telling you what you're missing.

Company pages

LinkedIn also offers the option of creating a *company page*. These pages, as their name suggests, are designed to profile a company rather than an individual.

Encourage your boss to take a few minutes to create a business profile. LinkedIn participants will then be encouraged to follow your company page to learn more about what you do. Like personal pages, company pages can include links to videos demonstrating how unique products and services can be used in the field. These videos don't have to be expensive corporate productions; they can be organic from-the-field videos shot on a modern Smartphone.

The company page is another excellent example of creating inbound leads. I have received several emails from potential customers who initiated contact after following my company page. I post **THE PROSALESGUY BLOG** on my **PROSALESGUY TRAINING** company page to provide followers with information on sales techniques and insight.

What can you share on your company page?

LinkedIn groups

 LinkedIn groups are communities of individual professionals who are either related by their field of work or share an interest in a common subject. These groups represent great opportunity for you to gain new connections and reach out to new potential customers. Do you sell organizational software for accounting firms? Join a group of accountants on LinkedIn and add meaningfully to the conversation. Again, the rules of social etiquette apply. *Stop Selling!*

Don't miss out on this

You can search out groups dedicated to all types of industries and professionals. Join the groups you like and share blog posts or interesting articles you find online. Post your own comments on the article and ask for dialogue and opinion. Comment on other people's posts. *You get noticed by sharing and expressing your opinion.* You don't need to be an expert. You just need to be authentic.

THE SALES FLOOR

You can even create your own group! Next time you're on LinkedIn, check out a group called **THE SALES FLOOR**. I created it to provide busy Professional Salespeople, sales managers and business owners an easy way to access valuable insight, training and information *free of charge.* I post articles from leading publications like the Harvard Business Review, Fortune Magazine, Hubspot and Mashable. It's about education and helping salespeople improve their skill set – even if their employer doesn't have the budget for sales training.

On **THE SALES FLOOR**, group members become motivated by my sincerity in helping them improve. I'm not asking for anything in return. They see the group for what it is – an opportunity to gain sales and business insight with a commitment of just 10 minutes per week.

Often, group members will reach out to me, view my profile and send an invitation to connect. I accept and reach back out to them with a personal message. I encourage them to post their own articles on **THE SALES FLOOR** and to comment on anything they read.

Do you think this might attract decision-makers to want to talk with me?

Do you think this encourages salespeople to tell their management to consider my services?

Do you think the group members who reach out to me could be qualified prospects for my sales training services?

Respond to invitations and messages

LinkedIn sends you an email every time you receive a message or notification. Make an effort to respond quickly, and remember to practise social media etiquette!

A note for Gmail users

If you use a Gmail account, these notifications will arrive in your Social folder by default. To ensure they arrive in your inbox, go into your Social folder and click and drag one of the LinkedIn messages into your primary folder. Gmail will ask if you want to do this automatically for future emails from LinkedIn. Click yes.

My daily LinkedIn practice

1. I open the Home Page and comment on at least one interesting post that suits my occupation, positioning or imaging I wish to represent. I make an insightful comment *without* attempting to promote or sell anything. This often drives people to my LinkedIn Profile and has created inbound marketing for me.

2. I click the *Who's Viewed Your Profile* tab in the navigation bar. I can easily see who was curious to click my profile.

3. I send them an invitation and make reference to something I noticed in their profile.

4. When they accept my invitation, I send them a message like this.

    Happy to connect with you (name!) Please let me know if there's anything I can do to assist you. Given your background, you might be interested in a group I created on LinkedIn called THE SALES FLOOR. It provides quick access to sales and business insight for busy professionals. Here's a link. Thanks (name)!

Professional Salespeople have self-discipline. LinkedIn is part of mine.

"I don't have the time"

 Yes you do. Everyone has the time if they make finding that time a priority. Please understand that procrastination is a conscious decision. LinkedIn is one of the most powerful online tools for Professional Salespeople. Give it the respect it deserves and you will see your return on investment.

CHAPTER 39
How to Use Twitter

 Twitter is another of my favourite social media applications for Professional Salespeople. It started in 2006 and is really a form of micro-blogging. The 140-character maximum per tweet means you don't have to be a professional writer capable of incredible prose. If you can send a text message on your cell phone, you can tweet.

Fast, immediate and instant

No one does instant better than Twitter. News breaks on Twitter. Social uprisings, earthquakes and other emergencies are first reported in real time on Twitter. Celebrities use Twitter to engage with their fans and, increasingly, to get themselves in hot water for their inappropriate comments. Law enforcement officials use Twitter to communicate urgent, timely messages. *Twitter serves the public interest.*

Business application

Twitter's ability to get a message out instantly – with an image – is a natural extension of marketing, advertising and imaging. A link can be inserted into your tweet for added impact and integration with other online communications, such as your website or blog.

Twitter is also great for interacting with your customers, whether they wish to commend you for great service or report a bad customer experience.

Say what?

Yes, I said a *bad* customer experience. People love to post their horror stories on Twitter – and that's a good thing!

Twitter can be great for dealing with these negative customer experiences. Every company makes the occasional slip-up that it would love to take back and do over. It's unfortunate when they happen, but they do happen. So what do you do when it does?

Erase a bad customer experience with great service by solving the problem.

Let that be the story your customers talk, tweet and blog about.

The key is to acknowledge the negative tweet – not *distance* your company from it. Once acknowledged, attempt to take the issue offline to deal with it directly. The fact that Twitter allows you to respond so quickly is one of its greatest strengths.

Of course, in order to respond to tweets about you or your company you have to know when you're mentioned in a tweet, right? It's easy. Simply type in specific key words (such as your name or your company's name) in the Twitter search engine (it looks like a magnifying glass). No need to even put in a hashtag or @ symbol. The search engine will display any tweets mentioning those keywords.

Twitter followers

The goal of Twitter is to accumulate a large group of great followers. The key to great followers is great content. Once you've amassed a large following, your ability to influence people will get you noticed. It's a courtesy to follow the people who follow you. Just be careful to check out their profile first and ensure you understand who you're following.

How to gain followers

Follow like-minded people. When someone who has a profile similar to yours follows you, check out their followers and follow them. You'll find many of them eager to return the favor. It's amazing how this one simple tip can increase your followers in a big way.

The re-tweet

Not sure what to tweet about? Start by re-tweeting other people's tweets that are worth endorsing. Add your own personal comments to encourage people to follow you through engagement.

What should Professional Salespeople tweet about?

 What image or personality do you wish to portray? For me, it's all about being a *resource*. I feel my job on Twitter is to educate people about business, sales and marketing. I use Twitter to publicize **THE PROSALESGUY BLOG**. Each week, I send out at least 20 tweets with a link to my blog. If you read my blog, you might check out other areas of my website. If you check out other areas of my website, you might become interested in my services.

I tweet links to great articles I find on the leading business websites, and I interact with Professional Salespeople, sales managers and business owners who might have a question or want my opinion. I also tweet links to **THE SALES FLOOR** on LinkedIn, which is another extension of my brand.

Exposure

Twitter can give you massive exposure to a targeted audience. Be consistent with your tweets and ensure you keep your market in mind. It doesn't always have to be business either – if you have specific interests like vintage cars, sci-fi movies or technology, tweeting about your passions shows your personality. People like to do business with other people – and other people have personalities.

Hashtags

A hashtag (#) allows you to target your audience based on *topic* or *geographic area*. When tweeting, use specific hashtags focusing on your target market and cities of geographic influence. Hashtags are a great way of categorizing your tweets and making them searchable.

Photos

People love images. The photo gallery of any website tends to be a major traffic centre, and Twitter is no different. We live in a fast-paced society in which people want instant gratification. In this context, the right picture is worth 20,000 words.

Self-promotion on Twitter

Is it smart business for Professional Salespeople to use Twitter to publicize products and services for sale?

Yes, in moderation

 Just make sure that's not at *all* you're tweeting about. The rules of social etiquette are just as applicable on Twitter as they are on Facebook, Google+, LinkedIn and any other social media application.

Promoting events

Not long ago I attended an art fair that displayed the creative work of local artists. Each artist had their own tent featuring their best work, and the event was excellent. The fact that I stumbled across the art fair at all, though, was pure accident.

As such, I spent part of the afternoon educating the local artists on the power of Twitter in promoting their product and future art fairs. Imagine how easy it would have been to take a picture of their art and tweet it with a geographical hashtag. A tweet like that takes two minutes to send and is free!

Needless to say, Twitter offers great free marketing opportunities for such events.

Your smartphone

 Your smartphone is an amazing tool that offers incredible convenience when it comes to social media. It's as easy as taking a picture on your phone and sending it to Twitter along with your brief message. Imagine the power of these applications for Professional Salespeople . . .

A Professional Automotive Salesperson takes a trade-in after selling a customer a new car. It's a five-year old pre-owned sports car in immaculate condition with low mileage. He'd like to locate a buyer quickly and make two sales instead of just one. Tweet it with a photo!

A Realtor just sold a house to a new client whose current home needs to sell in 60 days. The owners have priced to sell and are highly motivated. Tweet it with a photo!

A media account executive has sold a business owner a live, on-location broadcast for a big sale event. The business is donating a portion of each product purchased to a well-deserving local charity. The radio station personality is high atop a crane, asking people to stop by and make a donation so she can be lowered down. It's a beautiful day and the parking lot is full of people. Tweet it with a photo!

Get Creative!

Twitter really is one of the simplest, most amazing marketing and branding tools for your business. And here's the best part: it costs you nothing! *Can you really afford to pass up?*

CHAPTER 40
How to Use YouTube

YouTube is much more than what your kids watch for mind-numbing entertainment. Created in 2005 as a video-sharing website, YouTube can be a great tool for salespeople and other professionals. Videos can be uploaded and tagged with specific keywords that will create a more distinct video footprint for your company and further establish your reputation as a Professional Salesperson.

YouTube is owned by Google. There should be no surprise that YouTube videos are often indexed at the top of Google's search results page. Using YouTube will greatly improve your SEO and your ability to be found online. For this reason, it's an application worth exploring.

Tell me – show me

 In terms of marketing, YouTube is designed to visually display your products and services. It also offers a great way for Professional Salespeople to give viewers an explanation of how their product or service works. It's also very effective in illustrating your expertise when selling intangibles where *you* are a major part of the buying decision.

Your YouTube channel

Feel free to check out my YouTube channel – **Dave Warawa PROSALESGUY**. A channel is like having your own private television station where you can post your videos. These videos can inform and educate your audience on what you have to offer and why customers should do business with you.

Your own videos

Don't shy away from making your own videos. Professional Salespeople who want to be market leaders in their industry have to *go big or go home*. Do you have a product that is uniquely different from that of your competitors? YouTube is a perfect venue for it. Creating powerful videos, I should add, doesn't have to require a massive investment on your part.

$200 – all in

As I mentioned in previous chapter, I purchased a 1080-pixel HD webcam, two great desk lamps for lighting and some video editing software for a total investment of just $200.

Consider that, when customers view your videos, they are already starting a potential relationship with you. Many will view your videos in an effort to establish your sincerity and credibility. Many more will simply be searching for information – such as a video tutorial – on your product and will be introduced to your expertise through your video. *Why wouldn't you want to take advantage of that opportunity?*

Not only do I have videos about my training programs and services, I also reach out to my clients by posting videos such as:

How do you get the best results from sales training?

The ABCs of Sales are not what you think.

*What makes **PROSALESGUY TRAINING** unique?*

If you'd like to watch any of those videos, you can find them on my YouTube channel. Just go to youtube.com and search for **Dave Warawa PROSALESGUY**.

Leverage your videos

Whenever I post a new video to YouTube, I also link to it from my website, and social media profiles to maximize their reach.

Practise, Practise, Practise

When creating a video, it's hugely important that you are sincere and really try to relate to your viewers. A forced, scripted delivery is instantly recognizable and is just as instantly a turn-off to most viewers. Picture the camera as another person to whom you're talking. Use everyday language and don't read a script. Don't be obsessed about making a perfect delivery, and remember to pause every once in a while for pacing and emphasis.

Be conversational and real

Don't make claims or promises you can't keep. As you continue to create more videos, you'll learn to relax and simply be yourself. Your videos should be short – up to two minutes in length. No one wants to watch a documentary on you.

 Finally, always keep in mind the *context* of your video. Who will be watching it, what will they want to get out of it and what do *you* want to get out of it? It's also a good idea to have a *call to action* at the end of each video that makes an offer or simply tells viewers what you'd like them to do next (go to your website, email you their questions, etc).

Once you've begun to grow your online reputation by establishing profiles on Facebook, Google+, LinkedIn, Twitter and YouTube, you're well on your way to becoming a trusted leader in your field – especially within your geographic area. There's now just one other online topic I'd like to cover that will put your online presence over the top!

CHAPTER 41
Blogging to Attract Clients

Blogging is another great marketing tool for Professional Salespeople. It's a great way for your customers to engage with you and it clearly establishes you as a thought leader in your industry.

I've been writing **THE PROSALESGUY BLOG** every week since launching **PROSALESGUY TRAINING** in 2012, and I love doing it. I've never struggled to find topics. Everyday observations in business, marketing and working with clients provide more than enough material to discuss. I keep an ongoing file handy whenever a new topic pops into my head.

The impression

 Blogging gives Professional Salespeople an enormous marketing edge. What customer would not gravitate toward the following salespeople?

- *The Realtor who blogs about the latest housing market prices in your community.*

- *A Professional Salesperson at a cellular store who gives you the latest updates on new gadgets.*

- *A consultant at an office supply company who blogs about tips for turning a small bedroom into a home office.*

- *An investment advisor who offers her latest stock picks, reviews the performance of her last choices and offers a market overview.*

Why do we gravitate toward these salespeople? Because we perceive them to be experts and respect them for sharing freely of their knowledge.

Once again, content is king!

- Very few, if any, customers are encouraged by a free market evaluation of their home.

- A blog full of sale items is nothing more than an e-flyer.

- No one wants to reach out to sales apes who constantly beat their chests on how great they are.

 Impress potential customers with your expertise and knowledge. Earn credibility and trust based on your sincerity to help them, *not* your desire to make your monthly quota and earn a bonus.

Where do I blog?

Wordpress (wordpress.com) and Blogger (blogger.com) are two of the easiest and most established blogging platforms. Use their user-friendly, hosted interface, or get a web developer to help you set up your blog on the same domain as your website for maximum SEO effect. You can also offer to blog for the company you represent, assuming your company already has an established blog. Be sure to get authorization from your employer to direct potential customers to see you directly. If you're writing the company blog, you should be allowed some privileges.

How often should I blog?

Many experts will tell you to blog as often as possible. Consider blogging at least *once a week* and ensure your blogging frequency is *consistent* so your audience is encouraged to subscribe. They should be accustomed to new posts at set intervals.

Choosing a title for your post

 Ensure that the title of each blog post is enticing and offers the *best representation* of the story. Here are some of my most popular blogs posts:

- *The Five Success Skills of Professional Salespeople*

- *The 10 Biggest Things I Learned as a Sales Manager*

- *How to earn $150,000+ as Sales Superstar*

- *The Top Five Reasons Salespeople Stay*

- *The Top Five Reasons Salespeople Leave*

The title needs to be the hook that uses a motivator like the fear of loss, *"Do you really want to skip over this blog?"* You are competing for people's time in busy world. Your title needs to convey the immediate benefit of reading your post.

Ask for comments

While many people may read your blog, few will comment. You need to prime that pump. Ask for their input or opinion. When you get it, *always* comment back quickly. Think of it this way: someone who has read your blog has decided to *microblog* in return with a comment. Thank them and *engage* with them.

Share your blog

Make sure you attach your blog to every social media profile you have for brand consistency and to ensure maximum reach for your posts. You can link your blog to your LinkedIn profile on the LinkedIn home page for a powerful combination. Using Twitter, tweet a link to each new blog post, and share your posts on your Facebook and Google+ pages.

CHAPTER 42
Use your Professional Sales Skills Within Your Company

I'm always surprised, and somewhat disappointed, by how many great salespeople leave their incredible skills of persuasion on the street without using them within their own company. As I've told many salespeople at the companies I've managed, there is no sign at the front and back door discouraging you to bring your tact, diplomacy and sales abilities into your work environment.

Why does this happen?

Is it because salespeople are exhausted using their great skills with clients and have none left in their own building? Do salespeople simply not understand the power of having fellow staff members in their corner and contributing to their success? Or is it plain old ego that makes some salespeople think the job of the staff is to serve them?

We've all heard this before:

"If it wasn't for the salespeople bringing in the revenue, no one around here would have a job."

If you've ever said this, or even thought it, you need to check your attitude.

Give your head a shake

If it weren't for the people who are responsible for the product, you wouldn't have anything to sell. Everyone within the company has a specific role, and success requires a team effort. So please check your attitude at the door –

and correct anyone else who needs to get that straight.

The stigma

Like it or not, the staff within your building may have a *tainted attitude* toward salespeople. It may be based on previous experience with past and current people on the sales floor, or it could be due to some other factor beyond your control. It shouldn't matter to you. You have the ability to show everyone that you have class and work hard to secure business.

Consider this

 Your customers provide a buying opportunity and pay money for your services. Your fellow workers provide the service and resources that make you look good. *Why would you not treat them with the same respect that you expect back?* Your co-workers have the ability to either go the extra mile for you or throw roadblocks in your path at every turn.

Hey, that's not professional!

No, it's not. You would like to think that no one at your workplace would deliberately make things difficult for you as a salesperson. Yet they will if you give them the desire to do so. Do you really want to waste your time in the sales manager's office dealing with petty internal disputes? How is that going to affect your manager's impression of you? More importantly, how is that going to affect your performance?

Make a choice

Which do you prefer? Co-workers who talk about you behind your back and think of reasons to disregard you, or co-workers who actually like you and are willing to go the extra mile because you're a nice person?

It's really easy

Treat everyone at work with the same respect and courtesy that you show your clients. The occasional $15 gift card to a movie is a great thank you for anyone who goes the extra mile to make you look good to your clients. Buy a few and use the receipt as a tax deduction.

The most important relationship: you and your sales manager

Your relationship with your sales manager is one of the most important ingredients to your sales success. All Professional Salespeople have experienced two types of sales managers – the ones they liked and the ones they didn't.

Which one are you working for?

As you read this, there's a greater chance that you're currently working for a sales manager that you like. Most Professional Salespeople will eventually *leave their job* if they don't like their boss. In fact, it's the leading cause of resignation. It's a consistent challenge to be reporting to a sales manager with whom you're constantly butting heads, or with whom you never seem to be able to establish a mutually agreeable relationship.

If you aren't working for your dream boss currently, let's hope you at least have one that you appreciate, and who appreciates you in return. This should be someone you respect – someone who is flexible and willing to work in tandem with you.

Look in the mirror

If you and your sales manager are not compatible, why is it that you don't see eye to eye?

Are you on budget? Do you show your manager respect in front of others? Are you contributing to the overall positivity of the company?

I've always had a simple, yet clear statement to make in this regard: *"You are either part of the solution or part of the problem."* When management does its annual staff reviews, what do you think your personal pain-versus-reward rating is?

What does that mean?

A great mentor of mine once asked his management team to give every employee a rating of one to ten on both *the pain* and *the reward* of having them on staff. If the pain associated with someone was higher than the reward of having them on staff, they were typically seen to be *part of the problem.*

If the reward of having them as an employee was greater than the pain, then they were seen to be *part of the solution.* I might add that there is always a *limit* to the pain, even when the reward is greater.

Where do you want to be?

If you are consistently part of the problem, you are probably not a happy employee. Maybe not even a happy person. *Is that really how you want to spend more than 40 hours a week?*

So why work there?

 Don't you deserve to be productive and part of the solution at a company that is better suited to you? Instead of complaining about your current situation, consider your options before a potential decision is made for you. Much of your sales manager's decision to part ways will be based on your ability to reach budget and the vulnerability of not having you on staff.

When that call comes, it's very sad. We've all met salespeople who should have left years ago. Getting out now before you become jaded gives you a better chance of aligning yourself with a company whose culture and environment makes you want to come to work in the morning.

Your next sales manager

If compatibility with your sales manager is important to you – and it should be – then consider asking these questions in your next job interview:

- *How would you describe your natural management style?*

- *Is this sales position newly created or the result of a recent vacancy?*

- *If a recent vacancy, would you mind me asking why?*

- *If I'm the lucky person to get the job, what are you expecting of me in the first 90 days?*

- *Would it be OK if I chatted with some of your current salespeople?*

How will that go over?

The reaction you're looking for from your potential new sales manager is a confident smile with clear, respectful answers. Good sales managers welcome these questions. They show your character and guts to ask them. After all, they're going to ask you some tough questions; you're entitled to do the same.

Your relationship with your sales manager will have a large bearing on your billing and personal success as a Professional Salesperson. When you accept a sales position with a new company, there should be no doubt in your mind that this relationship will be a positive one.

CHAPTER 43
The Fastest Way to Sales Success

Professional salespeople understand the importance of having a mentor. A mentor is an important role model in your career that has many qualities that you respect and wish to emulate. Every successful Professional Salesperson can point to more than one mentor who offered them guidance and direction, and who made a lasting, positive impact on their career.

What mentors give you

 Mentors are knowledgeable, experienced, patient, understanding, well-respected and great communicators. They are leaders from whom you wish to learn in an effort to become more like them. If you truly wish to climb that success ladder, find a potential mentor and let them know that you would like them to accept the role.

A Protégé

 The role of *protégé* is less understood. It's not as sexy or bold as the role of mentor, and it's not often that someone stands up shouting "*I want to be a protégé!*" Yet accepting the role of protégé is vital in the relationship between teaching and learning.

A protégé is someone who is eager, quick to learn, hard-working, enthusiastic, open-minded, adaptable, motivated and goal-oriented. Most importantly, protégés are looking to improve their knowledge and skills by finding people from whom they can learn. They are looking for mentors.

The famous saying

Every good student needs a great teacher. Every good teacher needs a great student. Together they are like a spark and gasoline that ignite to form combustion.

Success isn't just about money

Success means different things to different people. It can be a high paycheque, an impressive net worth or the lifestyle that goes with it. For others, success is simply the respect and admiration of co-workers, colleagues, their employer or the industry they serve.

For others, success is even more altruistic. The ability to reach out to those less fortunate is a form of success for many people who wish to give back to society.

No matter what success means to you, all of us wish to climb its ladder. We all want to get better at what makes our heart beat and drives us to ever-higher levels of personal fulfilment. Here's a sure-fire way to climb to the next rung:

Be both a mentor and a protégé

 If you really want to achieve a high level of success, consider being *both* a mentor and a protégé. As you learn from your mentor, look over your shoulder. *Do you see someone who reminds you of yourself a few years back? Someone who is eager to learn, and who could benefit from your insight and* guidance?

You may have found your protégé. If you're willing to accept the knowledge of your mentor, you certainly should be willing to pass it on to your protégé. If not, then you should really take a good look in the mirror.

Lead by example

If you really want to be a leader and aspire to ever-greater heights, share your philosophies with your protégé and lead by example. You will become the product of your words. The credibility of Professional Salespeople is at the heart of their integrity.

The quickest and most sure-fire way to success is to be both pulled up by your mentor and pushed up by your protégé. It's the dual action of both roles that fuels the process. It's also inspiring to everyone on the sales floor and sets a great example for others within the company.

CHAPTER 44

The Top Five Reasons You Will Leave Your Employer

Staff turnover in most sales departments is huge, making many sales managers reluctant to invest in the proper tools and training for their salespeople. This, in turn, fuels the cycle of mediocre performance, low job satisfaction and continual turnover.

Many sales managers ask this:

"What happens if I train my salespeople and they leave for the competition?"

What they should be asking is this:

"What happens if I don't and they stay?"

The revolving door

 I've seen sales departments experience a complete staff turnover in a single fiscal year. The sales manager is usually quick to follow, whether by choice or by force. Attrition of key people is a big concern with buyers looking to establish a relationship with their salesperson. In fact, it may be the reason *not* to buy.

Clients can smell instability from a mile away, and it can easily scare them off. *Why would I start a relationship with a supplier who can't hold onto its salespeople? How long will it be before I have yet another new salesperson?*

Market demand for good salespeople

Losing Professional Salespeople is additionally challenging for employers as their former top performers become attractive free agents to competitors. Disgruntled salespeople with decent track records can usually find a new opportunity, as companies are always eager to pursue established sellers with experience in their industry. Very few Professional Salespeople can honestly claim to have stayed with the same employer for more than 10 years, especially at the start of their careers.

Professional Salespeople are proactive

In my experience as a salesperson, sales manager and sales trainer, I've found that Professional Salespeople will be proactive in one of two ways:

- *Building their business through prospecting, servicing and upselling existing clients*

  or

- *Seeking a new employer that better meets their needs, desires and future goals.*

The second example occurs when a salesperson has decided that he's unhappy and needs to look for a new opportunity.

The top five reasons salespeople leave

After more than 30 years working alongside hundreds of Professional Salespeople, not to mention being one myself, I've identified five major reasons why salespeople leave their employers:

1. "I'm not happy. If I were, why would I leave?"

Sales managers have to dig deeper to find out why their employee is unhappy. Unfortunately, most salespeople would rather leave than have that conversation. They feel that telling their boss that they're unhappy is the kiss of death. Forget your future, you might as well pack your bags. Talking openly about being disgruntled is a CLM – *Career Limiting Move*.

Sales managers need to create an environment in which their staff feel comfortable talking about their feelings *without* fear of repercussion. Before a sales manager says, *"They didn't tell me they weren't happy,"* they should ask themselves, *"How many times did I sincerely ask them if they were happy?"*

Professional Salespeople need to take some accountability for their own happiness. Ensure that you are doing everything within your power to be happy and productive. Play for the role of victor, not victim.

2. "My boss is a jerk"

 I'm not taking a swing at sales managers; I was one myself for half of my career. I'm simply trying to communicate a vital point. Salespeople overwhelmingly leave their employer because they have a *poor relationship* with their boss.

Sales Managers need to slow down and consistently think about their words and actions. All staff members, including Professional Salespeople, discuss the conduct of their managers with their co-workers over coffee or around the proverbial water cooler. Here's my philosophy for sales department harmony:

Salespeople need to be accountable to their sales manager. Sales managers need to be accountable to their sales team. Salespeople have an obligation to respect the title of their sales manager. Sales managers have an obligation to respect their sales team.

A note to sales managers: "Want to" versus "Have to"

 This is one of the most powerful drivers in any business or organization. If you can acquire the ability to motivate people to "want to" do something versus "have to" do it, you'll be capable of great leadership. The hardline management style of kicking butt will never be as productive as the leadership style of empowering people to want to do better.

The hardline approach delivers short-term gains with limited lasting results. The other approach makes a lasting impression long after your departure. It sets the example for future employees and strengthens the organization over the long term.

If you truly believe in leading by example, you foster healthy self-confidence and protect yourself against an out of control ego.

2. "I'm being micro-managed"

 I hear this all the time. Most successful, progressive managers don't want to run a day care. If they had their way, they wouldn't need customer relationship management programs, call sheets or access to your calendar. In many cases, they have to. It's a condition of their employment.

What they want and need are *results* on your weekly sales report. To over-achieve on monthly budgets, you need to have activity – prospecting, new business development, servicing and needs analysis. Run your sales activities as a business within the structure of the company and you should make your monthly budget. Assuming, of course, that you have a great product that's in demand and offers true value.

Make your numbers and your sales manager will get off your back. If not, tell him or her something like this:

"I totally understand what you want me to do. Hit my numbers and be part of the solution, not the problem. I get it. We all have different ways of getting the job done. Fair enough? If I'm part of what makes this company successful, is it so bad that my way is different than yours? Especially if the job gets done anyway. Does that seem reasonable?"

I don't think many smart sales managers would fight you on that. However, make one thing crystal clear:

 If your way isn't working, you have an obligation to follow the direction of your sales manager.

Sales managers also need to understand that they need to adapt their management style to the salesperson – not the other way around.

3. "I'm not learning anymore"

Every Professional Salesperson wants to get better at their profession and contribute to the big picture. Those who feel that their career has stalled will be tempted to leave for a new opportunity that they perceive has more to offer. Sales managers need to continually develop their employees with education and opportunities to advance their skill set.

Sales managers need to invest in training. Start by going to **THE SALES FLOOR on LinkedIn** for great sales tips and topics for discussion in your *next sales meeting.* I established it for many reasons. Professional Salespeople know that they need to invest in themselves, and they know that it's they who are ultimately responsible for their development. That's why they'll leave if you don't offer them the ability to improve.

4. "I'm not having any FUN anymore"

Though it's commonly perceived that it's management's job to make the workplace fun, in actuality everyone can, and should, contribute.

Sales managers who take their staff out occasionally to simply say thank you are always appreciated by their salespeople. If expenses are being questioned, breakfast is a much more economical option than dinner and drinks on a Friday night. Even a round of lattés one afternoon can go a long way.

If your sales floor needs some excitement, volunteer to head up a committee that plans fun activities designed to make feel everyone feel appreciated and part of a team.

Did you notice something?

You just read the top five reasons why Professional Salespeople leave their employers. Hopefully you noticed that *money is not one of them.*

I seldom see Professional Salespeople leave a job over money, *if they are being compensated based on their performance.*

I have, however, found that making a high income can be a very influential reason to stay.

CHAPTER 45
The Top Five Reasons You Will Stay with Your Employer

Let's look now at the other side of the equation. It might seem obvious that the opposite of the last chapter would keep Professional Salespeople fully engaged and happily employed. Yet there are other dynamics that deserve attention.

Here are the top five reasons why you will stay with your current employer:

1. You're making a comfortable living on the commissions you're earning

Income was an influencing factor in your decision to be a Professional Salesperson. That's why you decided to forgo the stability of a consistent salary. That's why you're reading this book! Your monthly paycheques are generally going in the right direction – up!

If dedicated hard work on your part is now paying off with high commissions, you are *not* prepared to walk away from it. If you've grown accustomed to a higher standard of living due to your high pay cheques, that could also influence your decision to stay. Unfortunately, money can cause some Professional Salespeople to stay with their current employer even if they are *unhappy* with other parts of the job.

2. You have a good working relationship with your sales manager

Your sales manager has many qualities that you respect and admire. You share the same basic philosophies, and meetings with your boss are not consistently painful experiences. You're convinced that even though your manager has the company's best interests at heart, yours are definitely on their mind as well. Your boss listens to what you have to say and appreciates your opinion. Let's be honest – this could easily be the #1 reason you'll stay.

3. You're advancing your skill set

 Whether your employer believes in investing in formal sales training or you're simply learning from the professionals alongside you, you feel that you're getting better at what you do. That's important to you, because you believe that if you're not moving ahead, you're automatically going backward. You feel great confidence and a strong sense of accomplishment in what you do. You've acquired some great knowledge and experience and are still hungry for more.

4. You feel there's a future for you with the company

 Whether it's a promotion into a supervisory role or maybe a management position, at some point in the future you feel there's potential for *advancement*. That advancement could be as simple as thinking that one or two senior salespeople might be retiring shortly and that a few key accounts might come your way as a result. *Yeah, like that never crossed your mind.*

5. You're having FUN!

 You come to work with a smile on your face and most days you leave with one too. Your company believes in providing a stimulating, positive environment where laughter and even the occasional guffaw can be heard. Don't underestimate the power of a happy workplace. I've seen people stay for FUN alone. We all want to enjoy the time we spend professionally in our careers. Why shouldn't we?

If you aren't having fun, what are you having?

Here's what we're *really* saying

 As a Professional Salesperson, you will stay with your current employer if there is more to *risk than gain* by leaving. While there may be some components of your position or your employer that could be better, generally you're happy – or at the very least content.

You would rate your position as being *better than somewhere else* you worked. Hey, you might even be happy – go figure. Why give that up?

Seriously, why would you?

If you're working in a position that you truly enjoy, do everything within your power to *preserve it* and *never take it for granted.* You're the minority of salespeople – one of the few not actively looking for another opportunity.

Whether you know it yet or not, you're probably even being actively pursued by a competitor or key client. Positive people attract opportunity.

CHAPTER 46
Your Future as a Professional Salesperson

When I look at my sales career, I recognize *four distinct stages*. These same four stages can be recognized in the careers of virtually every Professional Salesperson.

Because most sales careers follow a similar trajectory, passing progressively through each of these four stages, you can look at where you are currently and plan ahead for what's likely around the bend. No matter where you are in your career, consider the next step in your growth and start planning for it.

Failing to plan is planning to fail.

Stage 1: The uneasy beginnings

I remember it so clearly because I swore I would *never* allow myself to forget what it was like to start out in sales. If you're just starting out, my best advice to you is stay grounded, no matter what success you experience. *Remember where you came from.* One day, after you've all but forgotten what it was like to just start out, reach out and help a new salesperson who would appreciate your guidance and experience.

How you likely feel:

Unsure, frustrated, unaware, ignorant, silly, apprehensive and sometimes even *downright stupid.* On the up side, you likely also feel *eager, ambitious, enthusiastic, open-minded, excited* and *ready to work hard* and *learn fast.*

That's just on your first day! These emotions will continue for a long time. If you're in this stage of professional sales, try to relax and understand that you're in training. Luckily, you are on the job *getting paid* to learn!

Observe the successful salespeople around you

Go out on sales calls with them and ask them for their guidance in mentoring you. I have yet to see an experienced salesperson say no to this opportunity. Every veteran salesperson was in your shoes many years ago. They are genuine people who want to see you thrive in the business. Find mentors who are successful and respected by clients, management and co-workers.

What to learn from them

Take the best elements from every sales achiever and make them yours. Be a student of *observation, learning* and *application.* Be open-mind and don't look for shortcuts to success – you won't find them. Sales is hard work. Unfortunately, that's why so many people try it and give up.

Sales veterans make it look so easy. That's largely because of their experience, talent and established relationships. They too started many years ago with nothing other than *ambition* and *faith*, no different from you. Set your personal bar high. You'll never regret it.

Stage 2: The adaptation

This stage is still quite similar to your *uneasy beginnings stage.* You've been in the field for a few months, maybe even a year. You're still feeling many of the same emotions and probably asking yourself some of these questions:

- *What in the world was I thinking when I took this job?*
- *Why didn't anyone tell me this would be so tough?*
- *What am I doing wrong?*
- *Where's the manual that says how to do this job successfully?*

The good news

In the *adaptation stage*, you're finally starting to experience *some* success.

You're making sales and your customers are showing you signs that they like to do business with you. You just wish it would start to happen *more often*. The success you experience, however, is often followed by times when you can't even get an *appointment*, let alone a sale. You're impatient for more consistent results.

Continue your path

The *adaptation stage* will test your fortitude. You will only encounter more consistent success by having the blind faith and perseverance to continue your journey of learning. You're hoping to identify and repeat patterns that have led to successful sales and learn from the client encounters that have fallen short.

For each prospect, ask yourself:

- *Why did this client buy (or not buy)?*

- *What specifically created the sense of urgency for him to proceed?*

- *What can I learn from this that I can adapt to other situations?*

- *How could I have handled the call differently?*

Your activity level

I can't stress this enough: your activity level needs to be *extremely high* for you to get the experience of learning and adaptation. You need to be *very active* in cold calling, prospecting, needs analysis and presentations to be able to advance your skill set.

Beware!

I have a warning for you – take heed! *The adaption stage is where most new salespeople give up.* The eagerness and enthusiasm you had at the beginning is starting to wane and your lack of consistent results is taking its toll on you.

Unless you accept the concept of *delayed gratification*, you will be just another person who tried professional sales and quit.

Reach out

Continue to ask for support and guidance from your sales manager and the sales veterans on your team. They will smile, shake their head and tell you that what you're experiencing is exactly what should be happening. Your *character* is being developed through *tenacity*.

A football analogy

Keep your activity level high and a good sales manager will recognize your efforts without pressuring you for sales results. The sales you wish to make represent the *scorecard* of the football game. The right sales activities *move the ball down the field* to get you into scoring position. Just move the ball down the field and *get the first down*.

Get used to the *adaptation stage*. It generally lasts between one and three years.

Stage 3: The return on your career

 During this stage, just as it sounds, you're finally getting a *return* on your hard work and investment in yourself. You want to make this stage last as long as possible. While there will be ups (large new clients) and downs (client attrition), you are generally seeing *stability and growth* overall year-to-year.

Your confidence and abilities are the marks of your success. You've encountered many of the same client objections and are great at countering them. You have strong client relationships and the respect of management and co-workers.

Let's cut straight to the good stuff, right?

This is the stage where you're reaching a high income level. If you're doing everything right, you should see consistent increases with each new year. Your standard of living is rising and you're feeling pretty darned good about your situation.

You're now one of your company's senior billers

Your opinion is heard and respected on the sales floor and in your sales manager's office. The general manager smiles at you as you pass in the hallway. You're making the company money and get to share in that success.

Never forget to continue to do all the activities that got you to the *return on your career stage*. Do *not* become complacent. I've seen far too many salespeople settle into cruise control mode and stop prospecting. Then, when they suddenly experience a high level of client attrition, they have to leap into action with a major new business acquisition strategy.

The scramble

It can take 90 days or more to recover from that mistake, and those 90 days are not going to be fun! Be ever vigilant, remember the skills and activities that contributed to your success and continue to forge ahead.

Be prepared

Every Professional Salesperson in the *return on your career stage* is going to have great years. Save and tithe some of the money you make. Pay down the debt that built up over your developmental years and always be aware that there will inevitably be tough years. When those tough years come, you're going to ask yourself questions like:

"Have I lost my abilities?"

"Is my time up?"

"Are the good times over?"

"Was my success over the years too good to be true?"

Stop and think!

Did you work hard to achieve your success?

Was it the result of many long years of a consistent sales strategy?

Did you become successful by accident or by design?

Does anyone really lose their ability to be successful like a misplaced set of keys?

You haven't lost your touch. Dust yourself off and return to the activities and attitude you had in the *adaptation phase*. Look in the mirror. Set your mind to it. Get back to the basics and get the job done.

Stage 4: The so-what-now

Just as every Professional Salesperson will eventually arrive at the *return on your career stage*, so will every one cross out of it and into the *so-what-now stage*.

You've done well for yourself and are satisfied with your success on many levels. You can look back over the years and be appreciative of the many relationships you've forged with your great clients. Many of your clients, in fact, are now friends *outside of work.*

Much of your business is long-term with annual agreements. Your clients consult with you before making any decisions. You are what I call *on the inside looking out* with them. Salespeople at other suppliers are *on the outside looking in.* You remember what that used to feel like.

Why in the world would you do anything to change this picture?

Good question!

If the answer is "*I wouldn't,*" then enjoy the position you're in. You've worked many long years to get here. Make it last for as long as you are fulfilled and satisfied. There's no doubt that many salespeople look at you with respect, admiration and even some jealousy over your big accounts.

Looking for some new challenges?

Making sales at this point in your career is almost routine. You've countered every objection, dealt with every complaint and received praise from your clients. You may not be looking for any new challenges. If you are, however, there are several ways to go about it.

Team building options

 Ask your sales manager if you can head up some group activities that they would appreciate assistance with. Could you help train new salespeople, sit on a planning committee for a special project or be responsible for team-building social activities?

There are many leadership opportunities available to a Professional Salesperson in the *so-what-now stage.* If true leadership is a consideration, perhaps you should be asking yourself this question:

Is it time to consider management?

It seems inevitable that every successful Professional Salesperson would consider management. In actuality, I find most people to be somewhat polarized on the issue. While it appears to be the epitome of any sales career, the decision to join management (or not) requires serious consideration.

Those who decide to enter management have usually been enticed by the idea for quite some time. Other Professional Salespeople, however, are content to stay in their current roles, contributing to the success of the company. They tend to enjoy the benefits of being a top producer, and in some cases may actually bring home a bigger paycheque as a salesperson than they would as a manager.

Why enter management?

Here are the reasons you might consider taking on the role of sales manager:

- *You've achieved great success and are ambitious to continue to the next stage in your sales career.*

- *You want to take on a leadership role within the company.*

- *You respect, admire and feel you can learn much from your company's current management team.*

- *You want more responsibility and the ability to make decisions concerning sales direction.*

- *You want to be able to coach, mentor and develop talent within the sales team.*

- *You want to be a leader and be held responsible for the success of the sales team.*

- *You know you can make a difference in people's lives and be part of a bigger picture.*

- *You see sales management as a stepping-stone to higher corporate roles and responsibilities.*

- *You know that not going into management will always leave you wondering "What if?"*

Answer these questions before accepting a role in management:

- *Have you accomplished everything you wanted to as a Professional Salesperson?*

- *Can you handle not being the Sales Superstar anymore?*

- *Are you prepared to go into a new field that you may know little about: Managing people?*

- *Are you willing to re-start the four stages in a new role?*

- *Are you prepared to be responsible for the overall budget – which is everyone else's combined?*

- *Are you ready to give up your freedom and flexibility as a top producer?*

- *Are you willing to work harder than you've ever done before?*

- *Are you willing to lead by example, believe in salespeople and face their scrutiny?*

- *Are you prepared to be held accountable for the results of your sales team?*

Answering each and every one of these questions can quickly make your decision very clear to you. You may find yourself firmly on one side or the other, in which case it's an easy decision. If your answers are more ambiguous, take these questions to your sales manager and anyone else you respect. Ask their opinion. *The better the information you have, the better the decision you'll make.*

Only *you* can make this call.

CLOSING
Be Proud of Your Occupation

Please go back to chapter one – *The Stigma of Sales*. It will bring depth and meaning to my final words. If you've read this book in its entirety, congratulations! You've made a major investment in your future and I respect you for that. You are not a victim of the stigma. You are the *victor - a Professional Salesperson!*

Hold your head high

 You bring respect to the words **Professional Salesperson** and don't need to hide behind another title for the job.

- You *ask questions* with the precision of a surgeon.

- You have the ability to *actively listen and paraphrase* with the clarity of a courtroom lawyer.

- Your *integrity* is evident and clearly defined, with no shades of grey.

- You have mastered the most powerful human skill – *the ability to relate to and influence people.*

- You take the time to *help* fellow salespeople who want to improve.

- You are *respected* by clients, managers, and co-workers.

- You are in *training* every day of your career.

- Every presentation is a *performance* with a judge evaluating you.

- You have the potential to make more *money* than most people you know.

- You've applied your on-the-job professional skills to *guide and mentor* colleagues and friends.

As a great mentor once told me:

> *"Nothing happens until someone sells something."*

You are a Professional Salesperson.   Go do your job.

I'm always interested in your feedback. I can be reached at **www. prosalesguy.ca** and have a *SHUT UP! Stop Talking and Start Making Money* Facebook Fan Page link on my website. I would love to hear of your experiences using these sales techniques. You will also find a list of my 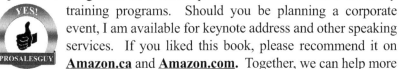 training programs. Should you be planning a corporate event, I am available for keynote address and other speaking services. If you liked this book, please recommend it on **Amazon.ca** and **Amazon.com**. Together, we can help more Professional Salespeople. Thanks!

62071251R00141

Made in the USA
Charleston, SC
03 October 2016